Thanks, I Needed That.

And Other Stories of the Spirit

To Judy — warmest wishes.

Robert Alper

Read The Spirit Books

an imprint of
David Crumm Media, LLC
Canton, Michigan

For more information and further discussion, visit
www.INeededThat.info

Cover art and design by
Rick Nease
www.RickNeaseArt.com

Published By
Read The Spirit Books
an imprint of
David Crumm Media, LLC
42015 Ford Rd., Suite 234
Canton, Michigan, USA

For information about customized editions, bulk purchases
or permissions, contact David Crumm Media, LLC at info@
DavidCrummMedia.com

Dedication

TO SHERRI

What greater thing is there for two human souls, than to feel that they are joined for life—to strengthen each other in all labor, to rest on each other in all sorrow, to minister to each other in all pain, to be one with each other in silent unspeakable memories?

—George Eliot

To everything there is a season, and a time for every purpose under the heaven:

A time to be born and a time to die

A time to plant and a time to pluck up that which is planted

A time to kill, and a time to heal

A time to break down, and a time to build up

A time to weep, and a time to laugh

A time to mourn and a time to dance

A time to cast away stones, and a time to gather stones together

A time to embrace and a time to refrain from embracing

A time to seek and a time to lose

A time to keep and a time to cast away

A time to rend and a time to sew

A time to keep silence, and a time to speak

A time to love, and a time to hate

A time for war, and a time for peace.

—*Ecclesiastes 3: 1-8*

Contents

Introduction

A RABBI WHO did stand-up comedy before 2,000 Muslims probably has a few good stories.

From his home in rural Vermont, Rabbi Bob Alper writes about growing up in Rhode Island, completing college and rabbinical seminary, and serving as rabbi at large congregations in Buffalo and Philadelphia. He was always funny, he notes, from delivering bad puns as a toddler to entertaining during teenage youth group retreats. In his synagogues, he regularly used jokes and humorous illustrations in sermons—so, as he tells the story, he has "years of experience performing in front of a hostile audience."

In 1986, living in a Philadelphia suburb and armed with a doctoral degree from Princeton Theological Seminary, Bob was charting a different path, trading congregational life for a counseling practice. But at that same time, comedy reared its ugly head in the form of a "Jewish Comic of the Year Contest." Bob entered, came in third behind a chiropractor and a lawyer, and went on to make stand-up a full-time career. He's now heard daily on the clean comedy channel of Sirius/XM satellite radio, and has performed in over 2,000 shows, from The Hollywood IMPROV to London's New End Theatre, as well as hundreds of synagogues, churches, mosques, theatres, colleges and corporate events.

Particularly gratifying to Bob is his creation of "The Laugh in Peace Tour," non-political comedy performances with Muslim and Christian colleagues. Juliana Oyegun, Chief Diversity Officer of The World Bank, observed "…your voices offer powerful lessons of reconciliation and understanding through the language of laughter and joy. I can't think of a more timely message for our world."

There's literally no other storyteller like Bob Alper, the world's only full-time standup comic who also remains a practicing rabbi.

In this book's 32 true stories, Bob writes about his journey and, in particular, the people he's met along the way: a brave Russian Jew contending with the KGB; a severely injured pilot; a deeply spiritual stained glass artist; an eccentric Englishwoman and her small dog; a grieving carpenter; a religious Polish prisoner exiled to Siberia; and so many more, including a cat named Dracula. Bob finds his inspiration both at home and during his travels, focusing on ordinary people whose lives yield lessons that evoke laughter and tears, often on the same page. And Bob reports from a wide range of locations including a general store in Vermont, a prestigious London church and synagogue, backstage at *The Tonight Show*, and an apartment in a gray Moscow suburb.

Though infused with Bob's trademark humor, *Thanks. I Needed That.* artfully, and sometimes unexpectedly, touches readers through stories of ordinary people: their struggles, successes, failures, and often, the unintentional and surprising ways strangers enhance the lives of others.

—David Crumm, Editor at Read the Spirit Books

CHAPTER 1

Find Me a Husband

IN THE SPRING of 1992, my wife, Sherri, was working at her alma mater, Bennington College, directing adjunct academic programs. One Thursday afternoon, she happened to pass by the office of her friend, Irene Rozensweig.

Typical late day chat, ending with Sherri explaining that she would be away until Monday. "I'm doing some workshops at a convention in San Antonio."

"Have a safe trip," Irene called out. And as an afterthought, added, "And by the way: find me a husband."

Irene, a Jewish woman, child of two Holocaust survivors, never-married, in her 30s, was at that time involved in a going-nowhere relationship with a going-nowhere man. So the funny, ironic request, "Find me a husband," was neither unusual nor unexpected.

But Irene may have been surprised just a bit when Sherri responded, "Irene: I'm going to a convention of rabbis."

To which Irene responded, "Oh—that'd be all right."

Two days later Sherri found herself conducting a workshop for 30 or 40 rabbis. One rabbi in particular stood out from the crowd.

Not surprisingly. Physically, he towered above the rest. About six feet four inches, heavy-set, bearded, what people often describe as a bear of a man. But it was his gentle, warm, bright personality that particularly caught Sherri's attention.

When the workshop ended, Sherri the instructor became Sherri the matchmaker, something she'd never before done.

"Tell me about Howard Jaffe," she asked her friends at the conference. And the responses were all the same. "What a sweetie." "A real mentsch." "A doll." "Thirty-six and never married. Would like to be married. Great guy." "His congregation and his colleagues all adore him."

So Sherri sent him a note: "Hi, Howard. I've never written a message like this before, and I don't mean to be intrusive, but after meeting you today, I thought that—well—I have a friend, Irene ..." and so on.

Later, Howard met with Sherri in the lobby.

"Sure. Give her my number."

Which Sherri did when she returned to Bennington. Soon Irene placed a call to Howard at his synagogue, but when the secretary answered, Irene panicked and hung up. Fortunately, her nerves calmed and she tried again, leading to hours and hours of conversation and The Meeting two weeks later. The following December, Howard and Irene were married.

Soon they began working on their most heartfelt goal: a family. But getting pregnant was difficult. They endured the usual round of clinics and experts and finally met with success. Success and success: Irene became pregnant with twins.

I'll skip the details, but simply report that the pregnancy was difficult, and the birth scary. Ultimately Howard and Irene the couple became Howard and Irene the family, blessed with a son and a daughter.

Sherri and I drove down to New Jersey for the huge celebration that marked the bris of the son and the baby-naming of the daughter. It was an incredibly joyful time, and Sherri was hailed for her role in the wonderful story, just as she had been, deservedly, at the wedding.

After the hugs and kisses, after we admired the gorgeous infants, wrapped in flannel and surrounded by all things soft, after we became reacquainted with the siblings and parents and cousins we had met at the wedding, after we ate a bit of the tons of food that filled the dining room, we sat in the living room, talking quietly, in groups of two or three.

That's when Irene told me a story.

Both of her parents were concentration camp survivors. Irene's mother, Helen, was liberated from Auschwitz. Her father, Izzy, survived Dachau, Bergen Belsen, and other camps. The Germans murdered their entire families: Helen's mother, father, and two brothers; Izzy's mother, father, and his four younger sisters. Of their immediate families, Izzy was the sole survivor of his, and only Helen and her sister survived from their family.

During the months of pregnancy, Irene told me, she and Howard debated which names to use, as all expectant parents do. A boy would be named Nathaniel, for Howard's late father. But a girl—for a girl, there were several possibilities: Esther, perhaps, or Sophie, women who had been important in Irene's life, women Irene knew.

And then, as the due date drew close, somehow, quite unexpectedly, Irene had a revelation: through all the years, it was as if her other aunts, her father's sisters, had been forgotten. Nobody carried their names. And so Irene and Howard decided, during the last days of pregnancy, to honor the names of Sela and Pessa Rosenzweig, two teenage girls murdered by the Germans, two teenage girls whom only Izzy Rosenzweig remembered.

And so the names were chosen. The boy would carry the name of his grandfather. And the girl would carry two names honoring her great aunts, Sela and Pessa.

Then something unexpected happened.

For fifty years, Irene's mother told her, Izzy Rozenzweig never, ever spoke of his sisters. Never mentioned their names. It was simply too painful.

But when he learned that his granddaughter would bear the names of his sisters, for the first time it seemed as if a padlocked doorway had sprung open, and the memories poured forth. After 50 years of silence, Irene's father was finally able to articulate his pain, to recall his sisters, and, one might certainly infer, feel a sense that these martyrs would be remembered always through the life of his granddaughter.

Irene and I drifted to different topics. Others joined our small conversation. People entered and left the room, nibbled and toasted, typical of a mid-size celebratory gathering. I continued to chat politely, but my thoughts remained far away, fixed on what Irene had told me about her father.

I was also tired. It was getting late, and we had driven many miles. I sat deep in a comfortable chair, and soon the conversation bypassed me as I pretended to listen. But I wasn't listening. I was watching. The voices became a hum, words indistinguishable. My eyes scanned the living room: people sitting, some in chairs, some on the floor, others standing. Frequent peals of laughter, animated faces, hand and arm gestures.

And beyond them all, the dining room. A table laden with gifts and platters of food, and beside the table, a new playpen where the two infants slept peacefully. Everybody had migrated to the living room. The dining room was empty. Empty except for the babies in their playpen.

We Jews are a people who know unfathomable tragedy. But what our history, both ancient and modern, has shown us, is that sometimes, after the darkest, most frightening, most destructive storm, there is always the possibility of a rainbow.

So this is what I saw through the chatting people sitting and standing in that crowded living room. This is what I saw in the background:

A dining room. Overhead lights out, the space dimly illuminated by the glow from the adjoining kitchen. A playpen with two sleeping infants.

And Irene's father.

He sat alone, in a straight back chair, beside the playpen. Leaning forward. Looking down, silently. Watching the babies. His forearm lay on the rail, and his chin rested on that arm as he stared below at the infants.

With his other hand, he reached down and gently, with the weight of a feather, caressed their soft, tiny heads.

CHAPTER 2

An Artist's Immortality

"COURTLY" IS THE term I would use to describe Tony Mako.

Courtly because of his precise speech and elegant accent, reflecting his Hungarian childhood.

Courtly, too, because of a deformed neck. Ankylosing spondylitis is what he had, making him slightly off-balance, leaning forward, as if he were bowing.

And courtly because, well, he was courtly. A gentle, even delicate man, kind, thoughtful, solicitous and unfailingly polite.

Tony was an artist whose medium was stained glass. For decades he designed and constructed windows that grace houses of worship throughout the Philadelphia area and beyond. His studio was located in a carriage house just down the road from Beth Or, the synagogue I served, and I met him soon after I arrived in Spring House, north of Philadelphia, in the summer of 1978.

At Beth Or I inherited a good news/bad news situation. The good news was that major renovations and additions to the old manor house the congregation had acquired began literally as I was putting my books on my office shelves. The bad news was that significant portions of the building fund money had been used for operating expenses the previous year by some officers who, naturally, resigned from the congregation soon thereafter. It was an unholy mess.

Into this borderline insanity walked Tony Mako. He had been commissioned by the architect to create the stained glass windows for the new sanctuary/auditorium, and one summer day he called my secretary to ask if he might meet with me.

That was Tony's way. Even though the building was overrun with carpenters and plumbers and electricians, Tony would never think to use the confusion as an excuse to barge in on me as others frequently did. He made an appointment.

He arrived on time, of course, and I greeted him with my usual, "Please. Call me Bob." After being with him for just a few seconds, I knew he wouldn't. Tony was dapper. Formal. And unconditionally respectful of the title rabbi, even when it rested on the shoulders of a person 25 years his junior. He was Tony. I was Rabbi Alper.

We shook hands and walked over to sit in the chairs that faced each other in front of my desk. It was then that I noticed how bent he was, how he sort of loped off to one side. I wondered if he was in some kind of perpetual pain.

Tony presented me with preliminary drawings of the windows he was to create. At least, he *said* they were preliminary. My suspicion is that what he showed me represented far more work than a rough draft, but it was his way of allowing me to add my input without feeling guilty. They were lovely. Carefully researched, aesthetically simple, graceful, meaningful depictions of the Twelve Tribes, Talmudic phrases, and central Jewish symbols. I could think of no suggestions, no improvements.

Tony fascinated me. It was obvious from our first meeting that although he was a wonderful artist with unique talent, he did not possess a typical artist's ego. On the contrary, Tony was humble, deferential. And I think I know why.

After getting to know Tony, after working with him on Beth Or's project for a year and consulting with him on his other commissions for ten more years, until the time of his death, I understood that Tony was one of the most spiritual people I have ever known.

Tony once told me that he had a nominal Christian background. But I think his actual religion was in his talent, in his art. We clergy help create moments of worship. We shepherd people through crises, both bad and good, and we have the powerful opportunity to make a difference. Tony created environments. His contributions will grace and enrich thousands of people's lives for decades or even centuries: windows of beauty and inspiration in all kinds of houses of worship.

He never expressed such a thought—that would not have been in character—but I'm certain Tony had a sense that for generations and generations people will find comfort and serenity in the prayer rooms beautified by his art.

He took his work very seriously. Day by day he constructed his immortality.

After Beth Or's project had been completed, Tony and I continued to meet. Every six months or so he would make an appointment to discuss a new commission. Usually he asked for advice about a particular religious object or a Hebrew or Aramaic phrase. Then he would describe his rationale for the design he was in the midst of creating. During those discussions Tony learned a few things from me while I learned much, much more from him. Tony began every design with serious research into the meaning of a Biblical story or a theological concept. Only after he had mastered the text and fully comprehended the literal and symbolic meanings would he turn to his art.

In all he created, whether for a church or a synagogue, Tony never departed from the absolute sense of holy responsibility toward his task. It was not a job; not a profession. Here was a man who really sensed that he was doing God's work.

Tony's face and respected name will quickly recede into obscurity. But the windows he created will endure.

And, ironically, this quiet man has another legacy as well, a living legacy in the person of his only grandchild. Strange to think how the generations meander, interweaving quiet lives with lives very public. Tony left his mark in houses of worship. His daughter's child is leaving her mark in film, and through life as a celebrity.

Her name is Drew Barrymore.

CHAPTER 3

Applauding New Beginnings

IT STILL HURTS to think about it. All these years later, more than half a century, and I still remember my baseball glove with sadness.

Like other nine-year-olds back in Providence, I wanted one badly, and though money was tight—money was always tight—my parents found the means to buy me an inexpensive fielder's glove that fit snugly over my left hand.

In contrast to a catcher's mitt or first baseman's scoop-like glove, this one had four fingers and a thumb. The "genuine imitation leather" was cheap, the padding minimal, and worst of all, the glove was flat.

You don't need to be a baseball expert to appreciate that a baseball glove should have a pocket, so that the player can snag those fly balls with just one hand. My parents tried to reassure me that my glove was fine. I just needed to stop the ball with my left hand and secure it with my right hand. I wanted to believe them, and tried to do just that. Not very successfully.

I was envious of the other kids who walked onto the neighborhood fields bearing hard-leather, permanent-pocket, sweet-smelling Ted Williams gloves. Sometimes, when my friends were at bat and I was in the field, they'd let me use their gloves.

Most nights during the fall baseball season I'd put a ball in my glove, wrap a belt around it as tightly as I could, and hope that in the morning, somewhat miraculously, I'd release the belt to discover that the ball had made a pocket in the glove. But it always emerged flat.

So I never became a good fielder because I never wanted to practice much, and I never became a hitter either. But, like all my friends, I did try out for Little League.

Here's what happened: I gathered with all the kids my age at the field on the day of the tryouts, nervously awaiting my turn. Finally, Bobby Alper goes to bat. Strike one. Strike two. Strike three. "OK, Bobby, that's it. Try again next year. You can go home now." Which I did.

A generation later, my own kids wanted to play in the T-ball and Little Leagues. Recalling my childhood humiliation, I was protectively cautious, but things had changed for the better over the years. While both my son and my daughter had inherited their father's athletic prowess, they still made the teams. *Every* kid made the teams, which is as it should be.

Theirs was an era of well-meant, sometimes over-the-top parental encouragement. I swear I once heard a father yell to his son, who stood immobilized in left field as a ball rolled by him, "Nice, William! You watched that ball *very* carefully!"

Most memorable from those days was my son's last year in Little League. The team was not overwhelmed with athletic ability. They had only one star, the pitcher, whose father was the coach.

The coach had a strict policy: every player was treated equally in terms of playing time. No stars. And no perpetual bench-warmers. The idea was to play baseball and have fun. And lo and behold, the team finished the season as second best in the league. The kids learned a valuable lesson from their coach that fall. The parents did, too.

Raising children, at least in our era, is usually characterized by years of ego-building encouragement, based on a theory that it's more effective to praise than to criticize; it's better to build up than tear down.

And underlying this practice is the understanding that, in many respects, children are a *tabula rasa*, an empty slate. We parents created them or adopted them, and throughout their younger years, we are continually molding them, establishing patterns, building memories, instilling values, developing personalities. Working from a clean slate. Launching their lives.

And so we recognize, we encourage, we applaud. "Great job!" "Well done!" "We're so proud of you!"

But in thinking about those parenting styles, I realized something interesting: we cheer our children's beginnings. As adults, though, we rarely cheer each other's new beginnings.

Let me explain.

For children, doing something new happens frequently, and we support those first efforts, as we should. But for adults, doing something new, or changing direction, is often difficult and even painful, sometimes risky, frequently the result of exercising enormous courage. And, for the most part, these are changes made privately, quietly, with no encouragement, no applause, no family or community support. Of course, people are lauded all the time for professional and academic and athletic accomplishments, for things done within the public parts of their lives.

But the hard work of personal change is usually kept secret, without public approval or support.

Perhaps it's time to see new beginnings in others in a different way, one that encourages recognition and praise.

There are models that we might emulate. In particular, Alcoholics Anonymous, and its sister organizations, Narcotics Anonymous, Cocaine Anonymous, and other twelve-step programs.

I'm pretty familiar with AA, because I live in East Dorset, Vermont. It was in our little town back in 1895, in a small room behind the bar of Widow Wilson's Tavern, that Bill Wilson was born. Bill became a successful businessman, and also sank deep into the disease of alcoholism. He and another Vermonter, Dr. Bob, ultimately co-founded AA, and now Bill's birthplace has become a shrine of sorts to his memory, visited by thousands annually.

Last year, on a warm summer's day, I was tooling around on my motor scooter or, as I like to call it, my "Hardly." I decided to ride through the East Dorset cemetery. It's a lovely and simple few acres, the resting place of a local boy killed in the Wilderness campaign in the Civil War, and a large number of children who died during the 19th century.

Toward the back of the graveyard, on the right side, one comes upon the Wilson family plot, including the very unassuming headstone marked William. Bill Wilson's grave.

It stands out from the others. Same size, but on that summer day, as on all days, Bill's grave was covered with small metal medallions of various colors. Just as visitors to Jewish graves leave a stone as a sort of calling card, members of AA place medallions on Bill's grave as mementos of their visits.

The medallions are in recognition of sobriety. Some say "90 days," others "25 years." All are placed on Bill's grave as a way of expressing gratitude to Bill Wilson for co-founding a program that has led so many to healing, a program that has saved lives.

Sobriety medallions. AA got it right. It's hard to make new beginnings. For some, agonizingly hard. Sobriety medallions recognize new beginnings, and often incredible achievements against a vicious disease with fearsome odds. They're awards, rewards, "'atta boys" or "'atta girls." They're pats on the back, just like the shouts of encouraging parents at a T-ball game. And who doesn't need praise?

Yet, for most of the new beginnings we make as adults, there usually is little or no recognition other than our own sense of accomplishment and hope for a better future. In fact, sometimes our humble efforts to change are misinterpreted entirely.

I read about a husband and a wife who fought for years over one of his habits that she found annoying: he would never remember to put the top back onto the tube of toothpaste.

This went on for fifty years. Finally, he decided one day that he was going to change. After all, this was a small habit to unlearn, and he ought to do it since his wife was always so good to him. So he began putting the top back on the tube. He did it for a day, two days, three, a week, and she never uttered a word. Finally, she said to him, "Dear, why have you stopped brushing your teeth?"

This little story about an honest misunderstanding demonstrates how, even when we try to do the right thing, especially when we try to change long-standing habits, our actions may be misunderstood.

On a more serious level, I was once witness to a quiet revelation as to how one man made one of those magnificent new beginnings in his own life, and how he did it, as usually happens, unacknowledged.

Sherri and I were having dinner with Abby and Vincent, local friends in Vermont. Abby used to work with Sherri when we first moved to Vermont, and her husband, Vincent, had retired a few years earlier from his weekly commute to Manhattan where he worked in the clothing industry.

Part of the conversation on that pleasant early September night centered on the one living parent among all of our mothers and fathers: Vincent's 95-year-old dad, Frank. Frank had a rough go of it during the previous months: he took a bad fall, was hospitalized for a while, and then entered a rehabilitation facility. While he was there, Helen, Frank's partner, as we say, the woman he'd been living with for 20 years, died.

Throughout all of this stretch of hard times, Vincent had shown devotion and care above and beyond, visiting his dad and Helen daily, driving them to medical appointments, shopping for them, and finding them help at home. Vincent was definitely a devoted son.

But what surprised us, and what Sherri and I discussed during our drive home, was one simple, unexpected statement by Vincent, in the midst of all the night's conversation. One simple sentence. "My dad was not a very good father."

Back in Psychology 101 I learned that many of the patterns we follow as parents, as spouses, are those we learn from our own parents.

We don't know exactly what Vincent experienced growing up with his father. But in his own life, with his own kids, he became a wonderful parent. And despite his childhood experiences, he also became a deeply caring, attentive son.

In other words, Vincent made some new beginnings in his life, working hard to build a different relationship with his dad, changing the old patterns.

Vincent deserves a medallion.

Yet Vincent's new beginning, like many, was part of a long, undefined process, with no specific start, no conclusion, no stunning moment of epiphany. It just happened over years and years. A negative pattern broken, combined with a radical change in direction, in style.

Other new beginnings are the ones where we determine to change: the hypercritical boss who finally realizes that she can catch more flies with honey than vinegar. The purveyor of gossip who finally understands the hurt he causes, and privately vows to mend his ways. The friend who finally lets go of a perceived insult from years before and now seeks reconciliation.

It's hard to make changes. It's hard to short-stop the ways of a lifetime, to break with those comfortable yet destructive patterns. And the plain fact is that if we do it at all, it's usually alone, without encouragement, recognition or appreciation.

Imagine if modern families sat around a holiday table boasting that their dear one reversed a history of parental neglect, or that their offspring, by strength and with the help of people who care, overcame a horrific addiction, or that their family member or friend went from being an abusive spouse to a compassionate, understanding husband or wife or partner.

Imagine if our community publicly valued and applauded those who made new beginnings just as much as we publicly valued and applauded our kids when they tried hard and took their small steps forward.

Imagine how much more eagerly people would be willing and encouraged to make those new beginnings.

Imagine.

Well, it's not something that will happen overnight, nor in our time, but wouldn't such a shift in attitude be welcome? And effective, too.

Imagine if we—if all of us—could hear these words once in a while from those we love, from those we respect. Imagine what it would feel like, after a struggle to change, if we could hear the simple words: "Way to go." "You're amazing." "I'm so proud of you." "You made a *great* new beginning."

CHAPTER 4

The Empty Swing

IT WAS THE swing, hanging from a tree in the middle of the yard, that made me stop and think.

A swing, with a worn wooden seat and long dark ropes attached to a high place on that tall tree, fixed tightly to a branch hidden by yellow leaves.

I don't recall exactly how the swing was put together. I never got that close to it, and wasn't particularly interested in its details. I only viewed it from a distance, across the roomy, open lawn. It just hung there, unmoving, on a day without even a breeze. A solitary relic.

It was early in September, a few days after Labor Day, on a morning that offered the first cool air, a foretaste of autumn and winter to come.

Sherri and I decided to take a walk. The moment we dragged out Sherri's sneakers and my hiking boots, our dog's tail began to wag furiously. He's a smart one, that Barney. He knows just what's going on, and for him, taking a walk is doggie ecstasy. I often tell gullible people that Barney is registered with the American Mongrel Association, under the full name "Dr. Bernard K. Feindog." He's a mixed breed who likes apples, so we define him as a Golden Delicious Retriever. Actually, he's probably part golden, part collie. He weighs 55 pounds and has an amazing bladder that will allow him to mark territory for hours without a refill.

And he loves to accompany us on our short hikes. Not that he feels cooped up. He's what I call a "free range" dog who comes and goes as he pleases, and has acres and acres in which to roam and chase chipmunks and squirrels and coyotes. But he always stays near the house, except when we take our walks. Then, like a teenager in a mall, he walks behind or ahead of us maintaining his distance, wandering off here and there, yet always keeping us in sight.

We took our usual route, heading down our gravel driveway and turning right on the town road. Woods on our right, and the big meadow where I cross-country ski on the left. Ours is the only house, but we pass a sign placed by our nearest neighbor: An arrow pointing east, up the road, with the words "Blueberries. U Pick." Within two or three days that sign would be replaced with one that read, "Sorry. Picked out."

Our road dead ends a quarter mile up, and we can either go right on Mad Tom Road, past the Wildwood Blueberry Farm and on to the apple orchard, or we can turn left, in the direction of the sheep farm. Barney is already down that way, and after he marks yet another scrubby roadside bush, he looks up at us expectantly. We relent, and follow after him. It's probably my imagination, but it seems he shifts into a victorious strut.

The road is quiet. One single pick-up truck approaches from behind us and the driver waves, then slows until Barney, taking his own good time, saunters off to the side. We walk past the swamp, check for signs of beavers, then peer through the woods to see if our neighbors, John, the gray-bearded, six-foot-six teacher, or his wife Ellen, the four-foot-eleven county judge, are out doing chores. Their yard, as clearly as we can see through the woods, seems empty.

Finally, we turn down Gulf Road. Hardly a road, really. It's just a driveway, even shorter than ours, but somehow it earned a sign and, I suppose, town maintenance as well.

There's only one house at its dead end, a small white Cape Cod that we know will be vacant. Not unfurnished. It's just always been vacant. Every time we visit the place. John tells us that it belongs to a retired university professor, his vacation home. Apparently, now he's too ill to travel from Boston to Vermont as he had done for so many seasons. A few years ago the man's daughter died. And then his wife also passed away. Dates and details are fuzzy. And, really, not that important.

It's the swing that is important.

The place is well maintained, watched over by local handymen who make their living as caretakers for those who have second homes. The grass is cut, and a riding mower sits at the edge of the lawn, either broken or ready to use. A stream flows right next to the house and into a rectangular cement holding pool, with three or four cement stairs descending into its shallow, murky bottom. The water then rushes out the other side in a small waterfall and into the woods below. We peer through the windows. The house is simple, furnished in country style, with plastic dropcloths covering the chairs inside and protecting the lounges resting on the screened-in porch.

In a small shed off to the side a plastic pool, the kind used by babies and toddlers, leans on end against the wall.

And hanging from the tree, one solitary swing.

It was that swing that so commanded my attention. I'd seen it before. Maybe I was just in a particular kind of mood that day. There's something so evocative, so energizing, about a swing cutting paths in the air, its occupant pumping legs, pulling on the ropes, watching the scenery roll back and forth. There's something carefree, young, lighthearted.

But not *that* swing. It was just hanging there, unused, neglected.

I wondered how long it had hung from that tree, wondered how many children had arrived at the little house with their families, raced out for a ride on the swing and argued over who was to climb aboard first. How many daredevils fell off and tumbled onto the soft grass below, how many exuberant high flyers ignored the call for dinner as they swooshed back and forth, back and forth, completely enveloped in their own adventurous dreams.

But that morning, the swing was still.

I felt a certain sadness mixed with resignation and, also, hope. Life goes on. It can't stop at one moment, much as we'd sometimes like it to do. The solitary swing gave pleasure, and for that we are grateful. And some day—some day—certainly others will own that little house, and new children will discover the swing, and their happy shouts and the creaking of the ropes will echo against the surrounding woods.

We hiked home, remarking on the newly-installed power poles, the reflectors strategically placed to assist the snow plows, wondering what the dog was chasing as he darted off the road from side to side, scampering 20 or 30 feet into the woods and emerging up ahead of us.

As we walked, we talked about the swing, about moments of pure joy so vividly symbolized by that swing at the little home on Gulf Road. We tried to figure out why the swing so haunted us, what lessons it was teaching us. And the answer came quickly. It was a lesson about the transitory nature of delicious moments in life, how they appear and disappear, yet always remain, sometimes buried, sometimes on the surface, as memory pieces.

It's important to consider, particularly since we're living in a media-obsessed society that gives us very false messages about the nature of success and the quality of happiness.

For most of our lives, the swing hangs motionless. Unused. It's still picturesque. It's still a reminder of contentment and joy. And, on occasion, the swing will once again give an exhilarating ride to one who cares to grab its ropes and settle onto its wide, weathered seat.

Transitory pleasures. But aren't all pleasures transitory? Should we expect life to be 24-hour ecstasy, and then pity ourselves when that's not our lot? Or might we be realists, savoring the high moments and understanding the nature of normal living?

Sherri and I continued to walk back down the road, toward our house, speaking about that swing, about extraordinary moments, and trying to place them in a proper perspective.

I recalled our first meal on Taconic Road in nearby Manchester Village, where our family built a small vacation home in 1984. We drove up from Philadelphia every month or so to check the progress, and one cool, early spring day arrived to discover that the roof was on, the floors set, and the frames for the doors and windows had all been put in place, ready to receive the finished products from the mill.

We phoned a pizzeria in Arlington, 12 minutes away, to order dinner. Zack, who was then 11, and I drove down to get the food while Sherri and Jessie, then 8, moved some equipment around to prepare a space for eating.

We ended up sitting on a stack of boards, right where our dining room would eventually be. We ate pizza from the box, sipped soda from cans, and gazed at the mountains through the rectangular openings in the wall that soon would hold windows and doors. Our kids were still young enough to believe us when we told them that Arlington pizza was the most delicious pizza in the whole world.

And that night, it was.

It was a special memory. We knew it then, even as it was taking place. We knew we'd savor it forever. Imagine: our very first meal in this house.

I confess that the mood probably lasted five minutes. I can't recall specifics, but my general sense is that soon after we recited the blessing and settled down to eat, one child became annoyed at the other over who got the bigger piece of pizza. Someone spilled a drink. I fretted over whether the builder would be annoyed by the stain the Pepsi left on the boards.

Someone wandered too close to the large circular saw, which stood unplugged but still threatened injury with its ominous, sharp teeth. No doubt we all debated over whether we should see a movie or attend an auction on our one-night visit.

That's the way it is with special moments. That's real life, and recognizing the nature of real life in no way diminishes joy. Rather, it helps us appreciate joy's true context.

Our challenge in life is to try to understand and accept normalcy, to treasure those precious high points along the way, and to courageously confront the trials and sadness we'll inevitably meet.

Which is why we can use a spiritual reality check every once in a while.

How to do it?

A walk down a quiet country road on a late summer day is a good place to begin.

CHAPTER 5

The Most Important Person in Vermont

"WHAT'S NEW IN Hollywood?"

I was talking on the phone with Ahmed Ahmed, a close friend and frequent comedy partner.

"Well, I saw Justin Timberlake in Starbucks. What's happening in Vermont?"

"A moose crossed our driveway."

Life in the slow lane. That afternoon a moose did indeed cross our driveway, then wandered about in the empty meadow across the road, finally making her way up to the Russells' home a mile away.

Celebrity sightings are daily occurrences in Los Angeles, but not in our rural state. More often the excitement comes from encountering a moose, a bear, a coyote or an occasional bald eagle, all of which have graced our property at one time or another.

Not that our tiny state is without famous people. In fact, the place is crawling with movie stars, authors, producers, media moguls, musicians and the like whose names most people would recognize. As to their faces, they usually sneak well under the radar unnoticed. Faces without make-up, floppy hats, and well-worn flannel shirts can throw most star-gazers off the track. And besides, with so much natural beauty in every direction, people's attention is focused less on "Could that be who I think it is?" than on the weathered barn hugging the mountainside.

I doubt any members of the paparazzi could earn a living here. The celebs keep to themselves for the most part, seeing Vermont as a place of escape, of privacy. Their second or third or fourth homes are mostly secluded way up dirt roads bearing no signs, although one well-known actor's home sits right on a street that's major enough to be paved. I spotted him one day, sitting in his car looking chagrined, as a police officer finished writing out his speeding ticket.

Caretaking is a major industry in our state. Local people are hired to check vacation properties during the long months when they're unoccupied, cutting grass, removing snow, making sure the furnace doesn't malfunction and pipes don't freeze. A few of my friends do this sort of work, and occasionally they share amazing stories of how this sub-set of visitors lives.

Art Tournet, too, spends much of his time serving the celebrity crowd. I met Art when he responded to my cry for help, a year after we built our post and beam, barn-style home on what had been a large, open meadow. Shortly after we moved in during the early winter, we discovered our unanticipated houseguests: cluster flies. These are the pests who appeared on cold days and congregated inside the house, at the upper parts of our large picture windows where the sun heats the air. Apparently they so enjoyed basking in the warmth that life could simply offer nothing better, and most of them would die at night. On a typical morning I could count 300 dead flies beneath one window. And we have many windows.

The next day, if the sun shone again, an entirely new crew of flies would find their way to the windows, slather themselves in Coppertone, and, I guess, acquire a tan to die for.

Time to call the pest control company.

Art runs a flourishing business, cruising around southern Vermont fulfilling routine assignments like annual fly treatments, or responding to emergencies, such as when the man fixing our hot tub discovered, deep in the guts of the machine, a four-foot snake. At least that's what I think he was shouting as he ran to his van and drove off.

"Hello, Art? We have a bit of a problem ..."

For the snake adventure, Art recommended that I put moth balls among the pumps inside the tub. It's worked so far, although when we use the tub on a dark winter's night, we approach it just a bit more gingerly than we did in the past.

But the flies required major attention. At the end of summer Art arrived, instructed me to close all the windows, and bring the dog and cats inside. Then he donned protective gear and sprayed the entire house from the outside. That winter, no flies.

Since then, I've looked forward to Art's annual visits. We're regulars on his schedule, plus, I occasionally run into him in town. Art's an interesting guy, a former teacher who reinvented himself by establishing what some would classify as just another blue collar business. I think it's much more than that. And it all goes back to the many celebrities who quietly inhabit these Green Mountains. Important people, every one of them. Some are salt-of-the-earth, others not. But what they have in common with one another, and with us locals, is they don't like bugs in their homes.

One breeze-less September morning, the best weather for spraying, Art drove his red truck up our long driveway. I went out to greet him and chat for a while before he went into action. It had been a good fly season. Good for Art, that is. Busy time. He told me about some interesting incidents with pest removal, and then shared a few details about work he'd done in magnificent homes of celebrities whose names I would recognize. But he didn't divulge who they were. Exterminators, like other professionals dealing with delicate matters, protect the privacy of their clients.

As we wrapped up our conversation and I was about to head inside, Art revealed another aspect of his unusual career. All those well-known people, regulars on TV and in newspapers and magazines, names that are continually hyped in the tabloids—they do want their privacy. And yet, Art boasted, "They all give me the keys to their houses."

"And you know why?" he asked with a grin. "You know why they give me the keys? Because I'm the guy who kills the bugs!"

CHAPTER 6

Creative Discipline

IT'S JUST A phrase in a song, but it's stuck with me all these years.

Although many people may not be able to name the singer (it was Gary Portnoy), just by reading the first few lines, most folks will immediately recall the delicious, reassuring theme song to *"Cheers."*

> *Making your way in the world today takes every-*
> *thing you've got.*
> *Taking a break from all your worries, sure would*
> *help a lot.*
> *Wouldn't you like to get away?*

And the sensible, comforting advice,

> *You wanna go where everybody knows your name.*

I adore that phrase: "You wanna go where everybody knows your name." I think everyone can relate to the value of that kind of a place, and, if we're lucky, we've had them in our lives at one time or another.

When I attended rabbinical seminary in Cincinnati, it was the auto repair garage. I had a high mileage Ford, which I drove 600 miles, round trip, to my student pulpit every other weekend. So I spent a lot of time at the garage for repairs but, more and more, just to pass the time with the guys down there, guys who knew my name.

They were real kibitzers. Once I reported that a valve seemed to be clicking.

"You have a radio, right?" one of them observed.

"Yes," I replied.

"Good," he offered. "Turn up the volume."

In Buffalo, it was another auto facility, this time a gas station a few blocks from our home. A Texaco version of the venerable pickle barrel. Our son was nursery school age, old enough to accompany me on my visits. He loved it, especially since he knew that as soon as he appeared, Bob, the best mechanic in western New York, would wash the grease off his hands, snatch Zack from me, and wordlessly lead him past the stacks of tires and into the car bay, where he'd buy Zack a Coke from the vending machine. Then we'd all sit in the office, solving the world's problems.

When we moved to Vermont in 1990, once again I found my *Cheers*, and it was in that place, oddly enough, that I learned a story about atonement and forgiveness, critical themes in the life of the spirit. It's possible to acquire valuable, enduring wisdom in some of the most unlikely settings.

Settings such as the East Dorset General Store, situated on the west side of Route 7, East Dorset, Vermont, population 685.

The store has been there forever, serving a mixed clientele of locals and travelers driving up and down the west side of the state. It's not at all unusual on a Sunday morning to walk in on a friendly conversation between a leathery, bearded logger dressed in muddy boots and hunting camouflage, and

Walt Freed, East Dorset resident who served as speaker of the Vermont House of Representatives.

During her first two winters of high school our daughter, Jessie, would warm herself by the store's iron stove each morning while awaiting the bus.

Presiding over the store, over this pleasant hangout, this town center where, well, everybody knows your name, is Ray Petry.

Ray's somewhere in his early 60s, thin, gray hair and beard becoming white, always dressed in jeans and a sweatshirt in winter, jeans and a T-shirt in summer. Born in Indiana, Vietnam veteran, former hospital administrator in Saudi Arabia, and since 1990, he's owned and operated the East Dorset General Store.

I go there a few times a week. To buy gas, propane, a half-gallon of milk, the essential cooking ingredient we forgot to purchase at the supermarket in the next town. And every Sunday when I'm not traveling, my dog and I head down there to buy *The New York Times*. Sometimes I find a crowd—meaning three other customers—and if they're local people, Ray always makes sure to introduce us to one another. If they're just passing through, Ray usually engages them in friendly conversation, although some sad people who spend far too much time in the fast lane can't seem to be bothered by such small talk with a stranger.

It was on one of those rare, quiet Sundays, with just a few customers meandering in and out, that Ray told me a story.

"When I was growing up in Indiana," Ray began (and many of his stories start in the same way), "we lived on a small farm with some pretty thick woods just behind the house.

"I was a decent kid. Never caused too much trouble. But I wasn't an angel, either. Who was? And as an adolescent, I pulled off some stunts that, shall we say, displeased my parents.

"Dad was the disciplinarian in the family. So whenever he'd discover that I'd committed a major infraction, he knew what he would do, and I knew just what to expect. He didn't even need to say a word. Just the look of disappointment, followed by a nod of his head in the direction of the small woodshed that stood between the house and the barn."

At this point I thought myself capable of finishing the story, and I made an attempt. "Going off to the woodshed" could only mean one thing in my mind: corporal punishment, what they call a good whipping, as if whipping could ever be considered good.

I began to commiserate with Ray over the child abuse he must have suffered, but he cut me short.

"No, that's not what happened. My dad was a clever fellow. He'd take me to the woodshed all right, but that was just the first stop. Inside the shed he'd grab this huge, two-man saw used to cut down big trees. Without saying a word, he would lead me out into the woods, not too deep, but to a place where a few large, old, and now dead oaks still stood."

A father and son purposely walking together. I thought of the biblical image of Abraham and Isaac, although Isaac was naïve, while Ray knew just what to expect at the end of this brief journey.

"In an almost ritualistic manner," Ray continued, "my father would scrape the saw along the bark of one tree, make a guiding cut, and with him on one end, and me on the other, we'd begin to saw.

"Now, a two-man saw is not all that heavy, and when the teeth are sharp, and two people get a proper rhythm going, the work goes smoothly. But when one person isn't doing his share, the other person's load more than doubles.

"With a business-like look on his face, Dad would guide his end lightly, move his arms back and forth, and put virtually no power into the task. It was all on me, and the work was hard. Really hard.

"It was my punishment."

Little Ray would saw and saw, struggling with the oversize implement, panting and perspiring while his father watched, stoically, from the other end.

Ray continued, "When I was nearly exhausted, breathing heavily, gritting my teeth, my body now aching, the sawing would begin to get just a bit easier. It wasn't that I'd become more skilled. In fact, in my exhaustion, my strokes grew sloppier. But at the other end my father would begin to do more than simply guide the handle. He'd start to add some strength to his movements. A little at a time, more and more, he'd join the sawing, until we eventually balanced one another, and the saw sliced through the tree trunk like the proverbial knife through soft butter."

Ray concluded, "When my burden became light, I knew that I had been forgiven."

A customer came into the store, paid for gas, and asked Ray for directions to Winhall.

And I stood aside, thinking about this beautiful metaphor for atonement and forgiveness.

Yup. Making your way in the world today takes everything you've got. Occasionally, by accident or by misguided design, we behave badly. Sometimes it's possible to learn a lesson or two about creative ways to obtain or grant forgiveness.

You can learn these lessons in all kinds of places, from all kinds of people.

Even in one of those familiar places, right nearby, just down the road, a place...

Where everybody knows your name.

CHAPTER 7

"Hey, Uncle!"

PEOPLE DON'T LEAVE footprints in hard cement sidewalks, but I bet I'm responsible for at least some significant wear and tear.

That's what I was thinking as I retraced the route from 89 University Avenue, Providence, to 141 Elmgrove Avenue. My family lived in that University Avenue duplex for the formative eight years of my youth, grades two through 10. All the houses were two-family rentals, except for the modest single-family house directly across the street from us. We thought the Worrels were rich.

At least once a day, sometimes more, Bobby Alper would leave his home, walk past three other houses to the corner, turn right, and continue another block and a half to Hall's Drug Store, 141 Elmgrove Avenue, where I spent every penny I was ever given, found, or earned. Plastic model cars and boats and airplanes. Sen-Sen and Pez dispensers, wax lips, and fake cigarettes that blew white powder. And yo-yos. Especially those hand painted models with fake diamonds. Once I entered an official Duncan yo-yo contest held in front of Hall's. Around the world, shoot the shoot, cat's cradle, walk the doggie. I did pretty well, receiving a third place patch to sew on my jacket. I never told my admirers that there were only two other contestants.

Hall's was also the scene of both the beginning and the end of my history as a petty criminal, all in the same afternoon. I was a young teenager at that time, and as I stood in front of the magazine rack, skimming through a *Saturday Evening Post*, I ever so carefully allowed a so-called "men's magazine" I had hidden within the *Post* to fall down into my open jacket. The observant young soda jerk busted me just after I left the store. My parents were not amused.

I recalled those days as I strolled along that well-trod stretch of Elmgrove Avenue sidewalk between University Avenue and Lloyd Avenue. Plenty of cracks in that old cement.

People who moved far away from the neighborhoods of their youth or early years know well how, when revisiting those now distant places, memories flood back, some familiar, some surprising.

It occurred to me while on that brief summer's walk, that during my formative years, Elmgrove Avenue was the scene of one of the most triumphant memories of my childhood, and of another memory, one of the most enduringly painful.

Jewish kids in the early 1950s didn't have a lot of heroes to shore up our religious identity. The Holocaust was a very fresh wound, Israel was not secure, and certain neighborhoods and clubs discriminated against Jews. At Temple Beth El we learned about the wacky characters of Chelm and schlemiels and schlimazels, and read stories illustrated by line drawings of little loinclothed King David using a slingshot that looked nothing like the ones we made out of twigs and elastic bands. The curriculum was less than scintillating, which is probably the reason I spent the greater part of my religious school career hiding in the coatroom or banished to the principal's office. I was not proud of being a Jew.

But late one Saturday morning, a transforming event took place.

Our University Avenue was a narrow cross street, but Elmgrove Avenue was a major thoroughfare, the route that ran between the Brown University campus and the football stadium. Every couple of weeks during autumn, two contending teams and supporters would parade down that street as we locals watched and sometimes cheered from our familiar sidewalks.

One Saturday—I was probably about eight years old—an amazing sight electrified me. I stood in awe, confused, exhilarated, and ultimately proud. Very, very proud. Then I ran home.

"Mommy! Daddy! You won't believe it! Brown's playing a Jewish college! Honest! They just marched down Elmgrove. A Jewish band, Jewish coaches, and a whole team of gigantic Jewish football players!"

My father scratched his head.

"Allyne," he asked my mother, "Brandeis doesn't have a football team, does it?"

"Not Brandeis," I interjected. "Another college. You should have seen it! They had megaphones and six white tubas and all kinds of drums and a HUGE banner right up there at the front. I couldn't believe it. A real Jewish college!

"Temple University!"

The second memory, though, is something I've thought about far more often. It's a testimony to how words—just two words, in this case—can burn themselves into a person's soul and remain there throughout a lifetime.

Hall's Drug Store was located at the far end of a small strip mall containing a barber shop, a market, a stationery store, a dry cleaners, and, strangely, at the near end, another pharmacy. Hall's was owned by the Rubins and was the Jewish drug store. McDonald's was the Catholic drug store. Hall's was busy and overrun with stock and carried toys and served lunch at the counter. McDonald's was sparse and spacious, with sparkling black and white checkerboard floor tiles and clerks who didn't smile all that often.

It was a quiet afternoon, mid-December, 1957, a month before my bar mitzvah. I was walking along my customary route on the way to Hall's. When I glanced up at McDonald's Drug Store, I noticed that John Baesler, a classmate of my older sister, Margie, and the neighborhood bully, stood alone near the doorway. We made brief eye contact, and then I quickly looked away. But as I passed by, about 20 feet from him, he yelled something to me, and I've never forgotten. "Hey, Uncle!"

It would be three years before I learned what he meant.

On my 16th birthday I did not receive a car or other major presents. Instead, that night, my parents sat me down to give me the gift of knowledge: a family secret. They told me for the first time what had been going on with Margie, my only sibling, two and one-half years older.

Of course, I was a witness to her tragically troubled childhood, the constant school explosions, the verbal and even physical fights with my parents, the police cars at our door. And I knew that at the time of my bar mitzvah she was in a private psychiatric hospital near Boston. I visited her regularly, at least during the first part of her hospitalization. During the latter part, I was told that she could have no visitors other than my parents.

On that night of my 16th birthday, my parents shared the whole story. Margie had become pregnant soon after she turned 15. Two months after my bar mitzvah, she had a baby boy, and put him up for adoption. By the time I turned 16, and learned the story, Margie had moved to California where she bore a second child, this time a girl, whom she also gave up for adoption.

"Hey, Uncle!"

Remember the saying "Sticks and stones may break my bones but words will never hurt me"? There's a great old Yiddish term for such an observation. *Narishkeit.* Foolishness. Of course words can hurt. Words can break a person's heart. The hurt from some words lasts momentarily, the hurt from others, a lifetime.

"Hey, Uncle!"

Why does this incident stay with me after all this time? It wasn't a lasting response to John Baesler. He was just an unpleasant kid, and I've never harbored resentment toward him. He wasn't worth it.

But I share this story, first of all, because I think it illustrates a simple truth: the power of words, the permanent effect, for good or for evil, of that which we say to others, as blessings or as curses, by design or just accidentally. There's enduring power in what we say. We need to remember that.

And the second reason for this story is because Margie's life was a saga of heartbreak and tragedy and also triumph of a sort, containing elements of misery, surprise, struggle, reconciliation, mistakes, and at the last, perhaps, somewhere amidst all the twists and turns, hope. Hope is energizing, sustaining, life affirming. So, perhaps as I tell Margie's story, some small sparks of hope will fly off and enhance others' lives.

Margie died at the age of 63 from lung cancer. A heavy smoker. Another "achievement" for the tobacco industry. A final, tragic milestone in a life so hard.

I won't go into all of the details of Margie's life, but among the so-called defining moments were her bearing two children as a teenager. There were other trials too, many others, during the years we spent together as children and when we established the foundation of our relationship as brother and sister. Those years were not pleasant, characterized by behavioral problems that plagued Margie all through her life. Which makes her successes, her small triumphs, her decades of what can be termed "normalcy," all the more remarkable.

In brief, Margie remained in California after giving up her second child for adoption. She married and divorced one man, with whom she had her daughter, Debby, then briefly married again. Her final marriage lasted longer and saw the birth of her sons, Kurt and Skipper. The family moved to Alabama, and ended up in Houston, where Margie spent what was to be the major part of her life, and is the place where she died. She worked at a variety of jobs, the last decade of her life as a babysitter for wealthy families who adored her.

All three of the children Margie raised are now married. One son lives in England, another in Houston. Margie's daughter, Debby, moved from Maryland to Houston, along with her husband and three children, to care for Margie, ultimately in Debby's own home, during the final months of Margie's illness.

My relationship with Margie through all the years was always strained. Every phone call, every encounter, brought back memories I wanted to forget. Including childhood flashbacks.

"Hey, Uncle!"

I'm grateful that Margie's illness and death occurred after my mother's death, especially so that my mother didn't have to bear the loss. But also because of the unanticipated blessing that happened when my mother died.

Distant all through the years, after my mother's death Margie and I drew closer, closer than we had ever been. It's not unusual, so I've learned. There's even biblical precedent.

The patriarch Abraham didn't have just one son. He had two. His favorite, Isaac. And Ishmael, the one who was cast out, the one who left the home to wander to other places. Isaac and Ishmael were estranged, but burying Abraham together healed them.

The same with the very different sons of Isaac. Jacob and Esau, intellectual and herdsman, were estranged, but they were healed when they buried Isaac together.

The same with Margie and me. We grew to understand one another much better, and in a very different way, at the time of our mother's death. Our relationship changed, and was, in some sense, healed. I am so grateful.

The change began during the days of mourning, which is called *shivah*, at my mother's apartment. As with many families scattered around the country, we needed to grieve and, at the same time, quickly perform the daunting, emotion-laden task of clearing out Mom's apartment, distributing 86 years of a life between Margie's family and mine.

It was three solid days of "Do you want this? You take it." "No, it means more to you. Really." "Are you sure?" It's a healing memory I cherish, setting a pattern for our relationship during the remainder of Margie's life.

The years flow by, yet I continue trying to make sense of her life, her death. I continue trying to understand my relationship with her, particularly my failures within that brother-sister bond. My hope is that sharing my story will encourage others to delve into and perhaps resolve their own relationships that are complex and troubling. And maybe, just maybe, understanding will lead us to forgive ourselves for our failures along the way.

During the summer of Margie's death, I went back to Providence with a heavy heart, now the final survivor of our small nuclear family, thinking of my father and my mother, and especially my sister. I anticipated that a walk past 89 University Avenue would lend focus and closure, but of course closure is a really dumb word. And no, my visit didn't help me neatly file away that part of my life.

I walked past our house. It had just been refurbished and was for sale. What we called a duplex in the 1950s had been re-branded a townhouse. I continued up to the corner where I had watched the Brown football team and their "Jewish" opponents parade down the avenue. Past my classmate Ginny Braitch's house, and across Lloyd Avenue. And there he was. McDonald's Drug store is long gone, but in my mind, he still stood there. John Baesler. Alone. Glaring, smirking at Bobby Alper walking quickly, eyes averted, on the way to Hall's.

And I could still hear the bully's throaty shout, "Hey, Uncle!"

Later that day I drove up to Boston to spend some time with a fellow named Jonathan Kay. Jon had joined our family circle about six years earlier. He met Margie a few times, has become a close friend of my niece Debby, and shared a strong, mutual affection for my mother. Jon and his wife served among the pallbearers at Mom's funeral.

Over lunch I told Jon about my visit to Providence, about the house, the street, the memories, the disturbing feeling that returned to me when I passed the corner where John Baseler taunted, "Hey, Uncle" so many years ago.

But most of all, we talked about Margie, about what her life meant, about what she had accomplished in her own unique way, despite getting a really ugly shake from fate. She was a survivor. Definitely a survivor. We tried to make sense of her life and understand it, as people often do when a person dies.

You simply never know where life will take you, what unusual and even astounding twists and turns life will bring. That's what we concluded, Jon Kay and I, as we discussed Margie's life.

As for Jon, he's a lovely man, very sweet and gentle, modest and caring. But read his bio and you learn that he's a graduate of Harvard University and is one of the world's leading rheumatologists, lecturing internationally. Through frequent contact with his Houston colleagues, Jon made certain Margie received top-notch medical care during her final illness.

You simply never know where life will take you, what wild and unusual and even astounding twists and turns life will bring. And so, one more thing. One final part of the story:

Jon was born in 1958, two months after my bar mitzvah.

I'm his uncle.

CHAPTER 8

The Pilot

WHEN I WAS a kid, one of my favorite television shows was a program called *Name That Tune*. Two contestants would vie with one another to see who could be the first to shout out the title of a song played by the studio orchestra, while at home, sitting in front of our 12-inch black and white TV, we did the same.

If there were a lyrics version of that game, the phrase "We know we belong to the land …" would present no challenge at all. Piece of cake. They're the first words of "Oklahoma!" from the classic musical whose stage and film versions appeared in the 1940s and '50s, and have been revived frequently.

While, as a kid, I never quite understood what "We know we belong to the land" meant (how can you "belong" to land?), I loved that glorious Oooook!-la-homa theme song. Even envied it, growing up as I did in a state whose best effort at singing its own praises was a college song that went something like, "For it's Rho Rho, Rhode Island, Island; Rho Rho, Rhode Island Island; Rho Rho, Rhode Island, U-R-I!"

After singing—literally singing—the praises of Oklahoma, I finally got to visit it years ago, and have returned several times since. With all due respect (which is what people say when they're about to go negative) in the opinion of this proud Vermonter, Oklahoma's not all that great. Flat, boring. Sometimes dusty. Let's just say it's not on my bucket list of places in which I want to spend extra time.

A few years ago I was driving from Tulsa to Stillwater. Speeding along the bland, monotonous stretches of highway, broken up by little towns and strip malls, I noticed that apparently it was clergy appreciation month. Because next to many of even the smallest churches stood large, electrified, portable billboards, proclaiming, "WE LOVE YOU, PASTOR RUTH," or "PASTOR RICK IS NUMBER ONE IN OUR HEARTS!"

It occurred to me that we Jews would never put up signs like that. But if we did, they'd read something like, "RABBI LARRY HAS GREAT POTENTIAL." Or, perhaps, "WE LIKED THE OLD RABBI BETTER."

Recently, I returned to Oklahoma, but this time I didn't drive down long, uninteresting stretches of highway. This time it was from the air that I saw the state, flying into Oklahoma City, where I did a comedy event, flying from there to Tulsa for another show, and finally flying home.

It's that middle flight that remains in my mind, the one from Oklahoma City to Tulsa. Because on that flight, something happened that was both amazing and wonderful and, at bottom, inspiring.

The story begins in 1973. I was a baby rabbi way back then, in the midst of my first year in a pulpit, following ordination. I served as the assistant rabbi in a huge synagogue in Buffalo. That's where I met Jerry. And Gerry.

I've officiated at hundreds and hundreds of weddings, but this was the only one in which both bride and groom shared a first name before they shared a second name. And so, primarily for that reason (but there were others), I remembered them.

Both twenty-four years old, Jeremy Cole had just graduated from medical school and Geraldine Toriski was a secretary. He was Jewish, from New Jersey. She had been raised as a Catholic in a mid-size town in western New York. As I recall, she didn't practice Catholicism. She studied Judaism with me, and converted to our faith before their wedding.

Gerry and Jerry, I should also add, were particularly lovely people. Warm, sweet, bright, and low-key. We kept in touch every few years: birth announcements of their two daughters and son; address changes and the like. We might even have run into one another somewhere along our different journeys, theirs to medical practices in California and eventually Oklahoma City. They were a good family, and a good Jewish family, too. I drew satisfaction from the part I played in their lives.

So it was particularly meaningful when Gerry (the wife) contacted me, asking if I would officiate at the wedding of one of their daughters, Shayna. The child of people I had married! Plus, it was not hardship duty: the wedding took place in Sedona, Arizona.

It was in Sedona at that beautiful wedding that we caught up with each other in ways much more specific than that which letters and e-mail allowed. I knew of their terrible tragedy, and in Sedona, among the festivities and happiness, many more details were shared.

Their son, Matt, always wanted to be a pilot and by age 23 had earned his commercial license. And then: catastrophe. A small plane. A crash. And fire, causing horrific burns. Matt survived, barely, and has undergone years of intensive rehabilitation and countless operations.

He is able to walk and speak. One can only imagine what kind of constant pain he endures. I met him for the first time at the wedding in Sedona. Matt has no hair; he wears a toupee. Both ears are gone. He clips artificial ears to magnets embedded on the sides of his head. His face is deeply scarred, greatly reconstructed. His right arm was amputated at the elbow, and he wears a rubberized prosthesis. The best the doctors could do with his left arm was to allow Matt to keep it, but his hand is permanently fused in a semi-closed position. And he's a nice guy. Personable, engaging, kind, polite, and very intelligent. He lives with his parents in an Oklahoma City suburb.

Gracious hosts during my return to Oklahoma, Gerry and Jerry had arranged for me to fly from show to show in a four-passenger plane rather than take the boring drive. We had brunch together, and then, on a quiet Sunday morning, they accompanied me on the flight.

Gerry and I sat in the back, while Jerry sat up front, next to the pilot. We all wore headphones that blocked much of the engine noise and enabled us to speak to one another.

But in the front seats of the plane it was mostly business, doing the checks and re-checks of the equipment and navigation, plus all the usual back and forth with the air traffic controllers. We had flown out of a small, private airport, but were set to land in Tulsa, a major commercial hub.

I will never forget that hour's flight, chatting with Gerry while watching the landscape slowly pass beneath and the clouds float above. We talked about their lives and mine, particularly about Matt's tragedy, the years she spent living with him and near him at rehab hospitals, the struggles, the accomplishments.

The flight was smooth and comfortable and totally routine. We checked in with Jerry and the pilot once in a while, but they were primarily occupied with the many details of flying.

Throughout the flight we could hear the confident, reassuring voice of the pilot, radioing the air traffic controllers, "Tulsa Approach, Tango 628 with you, 5,000 feet, heading zero eight zero degrees with information Bravo." And the reply, "Tango 628, Tulsa Approach. Descend and maintain 4,000 feet, turn left heading zero seven zero." Our pilot would confirm, "Cleared for 4,000 and left turn zero seven zero, Tango 628."

Pilot talk. Strong, crisp. Highly skilled. It was a small plane, but I wasn't worried. We were safe, secure.

And our pilot? It was Matt. Matt was flying the plane. Matt was in charge. Matt's was the sure, authoritative, calm voice of Tango 628.

I keep in touch with Gerry and Jerry, primarily through exchanging emails and reading one anothers' Facebook postings. Their older daughter, who lives in Oklahoma City, has two children. Shayna, their daughter I married, had a child, and the Coles visit them often, flying their plane, Tango 628, out to California where Shayna and Danny live.

And Matt? He's still flying, and recently achieved two additional milestones: he earned his real estate license, and he became a certified flight instructor, quickly building a waiting list of students.

Life can indeed present us with challenges, some more than we think we can bear, but also with the understanding that the human spirit is strong, that formerly ordinary people sometimes achieve amazing goals.

Tango 628. Matt confidently in control.

Soaring through the heavens.

CHAPTER 9

His Spirit Is Still In My Hands

IN OVER FORTY years as a rabbi, I've officiated at hundreds and hundreds of weddings.

And though I'm really not very good at names, given a hint or two—the time of year, the location, the couple's occupations and the like—I can usually recall quite a few details of each ceremony or events surrounding it.

There was a particular weekend in the mid-1980s when I had a Saturday night wedding, and another the following afternoon. The evening affair was strictly black tie, probably 500 guests, held in the fanciest room of Philadelphia's fanciest hotel, with coordinators coordinating the coordinators. The word "lavish" would still be an understatement.

Following the ceremony, the cantor and I offered our warm congratulations, which the bride and groom accepted somewhat graciously even as they looked over our shoulders to scope out the next guests in line. Then one of the coordinators hustled us clergy into a corner of the large room, still in our robes, and handed us two envelopes filled with cash, our fees.

"Count it," she commanded.

Which we, eager to make an exit, swiftly and obediently did.

The following day's wedding took place in the small living room of a Northeast Philadelphia row house with about 30 guests. The reception consisted of party trays from the nearby Acme Supermarket. The bride and groom, deeply in love, were surrounded by adoring families, all genuinely appreciative of the small part I played in their lives. It was one of the loveliest weddings I have ever attended.

You just never know ...

I always learn valuable lessons while preparing for or officiating at weddings. And not just lessons about love and marriage. Sometimes I become privy to glimpses into people's lives that teach me more than I could ever have imagined. Like the story a groom named Mark told me during a pre-marital counseling session, years and years ago.

We met in November, planning an April wedding that was to take place at his bride's parents' home. After some general chitchat, I began to fill out my information card, asking a series of important questions, an effective and quick way to get to know the couple.

Mark was 29 and Beverly 30. First marriage for him, second for her, following a divorce. She had no children. We discussed their religious backgrounds, occupations, how they met.

Parents? Both of hers were living, and still married to one another. Mark's mother was living, but his father was deceased. Beverly and Mark enjoyed close relationships with all three parents.

Usually, that section of the interview concludes quickly, and we move on to a discussion about the time, date, and place of the ceremony. But Mark seemed to want to talk. He needed to talk about his father. Beverly held his hand, and I listened.

Mark's father had died just a few years before, at age 49. An immigrant, the man was strong, a very proper European, not one to show affection. Yet, Mark observed, the man was very affectionate, in his own way.

Both father and son were cabinetmakers. For years, they had worked together. Father and son. Mentor and apprentice.

The father was diabetic, and Mark described in some detail the man's suffering, which included kidney problems, bleeding from the nose, and dialysis. And impotence. Impotence, which Mark's father revealed to his son on the day Mark found him in the cellar, curled up in a fetal position on the floor, crying.

Mark continued, relating the events of his father's last moments at three o'clock in the morning: the mouth to mouth resuscitation attempts, and what Mark remembered as "the taste of death."

Why have I remembered this particular story among all the others I heard over the years? Probably because of the poignancy of Mark's final words as he concluded speaking about his dad and their relationship. I've thought about his words for years, and can think of no more succinct example of spiritual immortality than Mark's very plain, simple, direct observation.

In preparation for his marriage, Mark was in the process of building a home for Beverly and himself, using the skills learned from his father. Of course, he was doing it alone. And so, Mark told me, especially at that time, he really missed his dad.

"But it'll be OK," he concluded, raising his strong arms slightly, and spreading his fingers. "Because, you see: his spirit is still in my hands."

It's About Time

THE COUPLE WAS nervous as they approached the counter in the town clerk's office.

It was understandable: they'd been living together for fifteen years and now, only now, had they decided to formalize the relationship. And they felt out of place. That wasn't unusual. My state, Vermont, had recently become a civil union destination, and thousands of people were making the trek from places like sophisticated Manhattan to rural New England in search of a peaceful, natural setting for their ceremonies.

The town clerk, the secretaries, the lawyers doing title searches, sized them up the moment they entered. These were not newly-relocated residents picking up a building permit. They certainly weren't stopping by to renew their fishing licenses or sort through the piles of Internal Revenue forms neatly arranged on a nearby table.

No, they were definitely your typical out-of-towners, nicely dressed in "country casual," here for a license.

The room grew quiet, and, while pretending to continue with their work, everybody watched with interest. "May I help you?" the secretary sitting at the front desk asked.

"Yes. Thank you," one of the strangers replied in a low, almost inaudible voice punctuated by a nervous cough. "We'd like to apply for a civil union license. My name is Jeff, and this is—ummm—this is my partner, Charles."

This was soon after Vermont had become the first state to permit same-sex unions. The legislature went through a long, intense, and, despite the strong emotions on both sides, basically mannerly debate, in the end crafting a law that fulfilled the Vermont Supreme Court's mandate that the benefits and protection of marriages under state law must be extended to same-sex couples. The discrimination same-sex couples had endured was deemed unconstitutional. High on the list was discrimination in healthcare benefits, inheritance rights, and the ability to manage the medical decisions for an incapacitated partner.

Jeff and Charles were nervous for good reason. Earlier that day, they had stopped in a different Vermont town office, where they were received with icy stares and whispers behind cupped hands. They decided to try elsewhere, and now stood in front of the counter in Manchester Center.

And as for the Manchester Center town office: Jeff and Charles would be the very first civil union applicants.

When I think about it, just during my own lifetime, American society has come a long, long way, and has grown splendidly in most areas of what was routinely accepted discrimination. In the late 1940s my parents nearly purchased a tract house in a post-war development—until the salesman realized they were Jews. No Jews, he explained. Their cooking smells are too offensive. We've gotten over most housing discrimination based on religion.

During my years at Lehigh University, so the story went, Jewish enrollment was traditionally capped at 10 percent. Three of the 30 fraternities were "Jewish fraternities," and it

chapter 10 • 49

was rare indeed that a Jew would be asked to join any of the others. That, of course, is no longer the case at Lehigh or most other colleges. We've gotten over most academic and social discrimination based on religion.

While living in Cincinnati in the 1960s, when I attended rabbinical seminary, Sherri and I volunteered with a group called Housing Opportunities Made Equal. Minutes after a black associate was told by an apartment manager that all the rentals had been taken, Sherri and I would appear, lily white as we are, and we'd be offered a choice of empty units. Then we'd make our report to governmental agencies. By now, as a nation we've made significant headway against housing discrimination based on race.

But our treatment of and attitudes toward gays and lesbians? We still have a long way to go. And while I don't intend to go into a psychological analysis, I do think our uneasiness is less a reaction to the behavior of lesbians and gays than it is a reflection of our confusion about our own sexuality, especially among men.

When preparing this chapter, I toyed with the idea of beginning with a warning that it really isn't a chapter for everyone. It's appropriate only for people who are openly gay, and for gay people who are closeted. And for people whose family members are gay, whose friends and business associates are gay, whose neighbors are gay. And then, I realized, this includes pretty much everybody.

Homosexual people are not "them." They're us, our family members, our neighbors, friends, business associates.

In a newspaper op-ed piece, the late Rev. William Sloane Coffin, former Yale chaplain and anti-war activist, wrote, "People who say 'same-sex marriage makes me uncomfortable' should probably remind themselves that comfort has nothing to do with the issue, and that, often as not, change is discomforting. I think that those of us who are straight people really need to sit down and quietly compare our own discomfort with the discomfort of gays and lesbians who for years have been excluded, isolated, silenced, abused, and even killed."

And he concludes with an especially moving challenge: "No human being should ever be patient with prejudice at the expense of its victims."

In that Manchester Center, Vermont, town hall, a brand new legal process was about to take place, and humanity was about to take a step forward.

The two men waited nervously in front of the counter, having briefly explained their request to the secretary. It's not a large office; voices at one end can be heard clearly at the other end, where town clerk Linda Spence stood pulling land survey maps off a high shelf.

Linda is what one calls "a real Vermonter," boasting local roots that go back for generations. Blonde hair, ruddy face, she's a hiking boots and flannel shirt type of woman with a no-nonsense demeanor.

Linda put the map down and strode purposefully across the office. All conversation stopped as curious eyes peered up from computers and town records.

"My name is Linda Spence," she offered. "I'm the town clerk, and I'm the person you're looking for."

Jeff paused for a moment, then said, "We've come up from New York and would like to apply for a civil union license."

Linda nodded her head slightly, looking directly at one man, then the other, during a very pregnant moment of silence she obviously relished.

And then she spoke. "Well," she said, breaking into a grin. "Well. It's about time."

As Linda prepared the license, she explained how everyone at the office had been waiting for the first such opportunity. Not only did she issue the license, but she also officiated at the brief ceremony right outside the town offices, beneath the state flag and the American flag, her office staff serving as witnesses and honored guests.

Linda was right. It's time to pack up our old prejudices, time to stow our old discomforts away forever, time to extend to the gay and lesbian community the same common, everyday rights we so take for granted.

Linda was right. It's about time.

CHAPTER 11

Joe and Justine

JAY LENO, LOOKING much more muscular than usual, sat alone on a picnic blanket, candelabra by his side, holding a delicate, long-stemmed glass filled with wine.

In the business end of a mammoth garbage truck.

It was a scene from a comedy bit that was due to air the next night, featuring Jay as a super-buff trash collector whose appearance on the suburban street acted as a love siren, summoning middle-aged housewives to race to the curbs where, bulging plastic trash bags in hand, they awaited the object of their not-so-secret desires. The lucky ones were invited to join Jay in his rubbish-filled love nest for an intimate dinner.

The video was hysterical, though about an hour passed before I was able to watch it in its entirety. Before that, it was start and stop, start and stop, as the editor tweaked each scene in collaboration with my friend Joe Medeiros. I sat on a high stool, looking over their shoulders in the darkened room.

I met Joe back when I was just beginning my new career in comedy. In the fall of 1987, a year after I had begun performing as a stand-up comedian, I somehow came across a list of comedy writers. Three hundred or so names and addresses, but the only local entry was Joe, who lived in the Philadelphia suburb of Glenside, just a mile from my office.

Joe worked as an advertising copywriter, was a musician, and had tried doing some improv himself. But his greatest creative joy came from writing and, in fact, he'd had some success selling jokes to a couple of well-known comedians and several lesser-knowns.

He was a lovely guy, quiet, low key. Married, with two small children. During the very early hours of each morning he would retreat to the quiet of his third-floor home office and write jokes for radio hosts and, occasionally, for comedians.

At that point, I'd only been doing stand-up for a short time, and, of course, I'd never used a writer. But why not? I figured if I wanted to make a go of this career, I'd better have more than seven minutes of material. So I called Joe, and met him for lunch.

We hit it off nicely. In between hoagies and coffee I described, and quietly performed, a bit of my little routine, after which Joe retreated to his study in an attempt to supply me with some material.

Joe would prepare a dozen or so jokes especially for me, usually grouped around several themes such as kids or telephones or sermon delivery. I'd read them over, select the best three or so, then nervously try them out at one of the daunting open mic nights at a comedy club when I was lucky enough to get a spot. If any of the jokes seemed to work, I would officially buy them. And send Joe a check for $10 each.

Occasionally, Joe would accompany me to a gig, where he could see how his material resonated "live," and at the same time develop new ideas. He kept his day job, but looked for every opportunity to write for additional comedians, from the famous to those like me who were just beginning to craft an act.

It's been over two decades since I paid Joe big bucks for the following joke, but I still use it in most performances. It gets a fine laugh every time.

"Being a rabbi and a stand-up comic is unique, but it was also predictable. Ever since I was a kid I've had dreams of having my own television show, making lots of money, and being surrounded by all kinds of beautiful, adoring women. But then I realized that would never work for me because I'm Jewish… and I could never be a TV evangelist."

It's a golden joke, artfully crafted, with the punch in the prime place, the final word.

Joe was really talented. And, like most creative people, he had dreams. He especially wanted to write for Jay Leno, who was then the permanent guest host on *The Tonight Show*.

One day Joe mentioned that Leno was coming to town to perform at the Valley Forge Music Fair. Joe was itching to get his material to Leno, but knew that most big name performers are surrounded by their "people" who ignore or turn away approaches by wannabees and unknowns.

Coincidentally, I had recently officiated at the wedding of Marsha Wachsman, the guest relations coordinator at Valley Forge. When I called her, Marsha graciously offered to place Joe's envelope of material in Leno's dressing room.

The day after Leno's performance, Joe called to report that at midnight his phone rang. "Joe," a very familiar voice began. "Jay Leno. I really like your stuff."

From that day on, Joe wrote jokes specifically tailored for Jay Leno, faxing them to California or wherever Leno was performing. Same as the Alper system, but higher fees. Leno bought Joe's jokes regularly. Eventually, he hired Joe full-time, and when Leno took over as the permanent host of *The Tonight Show*, Joe and his family moved to Los Angeles.

Within a few months, the credit roll at 12:34 am would announce: "Head writer: Joe Medeiros."

I just love this story.

So that's why I was sitting in a small, dimly-lit room in NBC's Burbank studios, watching the editor and Joe do their work. I had attended the taping of that night's show, after which Joe and I went out for a quick dinner. Now we had returned to the nearly empty building for the behind-the-scenes preparation that is needed to produce a television show. Exacting, creative work. Not very glamorous. And certainly not moment-by-moment funny.

Somewhat tedious, actually, in which a split second is shaved off one scene, an alternative camera shot is inserted into another, and the sound continually adjusted. I soon began to ignore the repetitious work I was witnessing, thinking, instead, about the meaning of those efforts.

And it occurred to me that when those three or four video minutes that were written, acted, filmed, directed, produced, and then edited ultimately appeared on television screens across the continent, predictable things would happen.

In one home, a father waits for his teenage daughter's return. She's more than an hour beyond curfew, and has not responded to cell phone messages, evoking parental emotions that bounce between anger and fear.

In a flurry she finally bursts into the house, apologetic, with an excuse that may be legitimate, and may be creative, with no way to verify. The father is about to begin his angry lecture, when the pair's attention is diverted to the television screen image of a woman wearing a frilly dress and high heels running after a garbage truck. Father and daughter suspend their tense conversation, watch the segment to its conclusion, and laugh together.

It's tough to make an instant transition from laughter to indignation. The father cannot and does not. Instead, a different approach. "You know, sweetie, when you don't come home on time, I worry about you. I was frightened tonight, thinking about all the possibilities ..."

Or: In a hospital somewhere a woman cannot sleep. The day's cacophony of caregivers and visitors has all but ceased.

Now alone in her room, it is a time of dark thoughts, the kind of confrontation with mortality she, like most people, routinely avoided when she was healthy.

The television flickers overhead, the sound turned low. For a moment, she glances in the direction of the screen, to see Jay Leno bedecked in a fake body-builder's torso. She turns up the volume slightly, watches the bizarre little skit, and smiles. For a few calming minutes, her anxiety recedes.

One could assemble a long litany of the sadness and misery, pain and fear that afflict all people at one time or another. Especially during the muted hours late at night, when the daily stimuli have quieted and, often alone, people seek diversion.

I watched Joe and his colleague place the finishing touches on the segment until it was complete, saved to the computer and ready to air the following night. A job well done by two professionals executing what was for them just a routine, everyday task.

And yet …

∽

Joe was on an amazing journey. It's a long way from Glenside, Pennsylvania, to Burbank, California. From a small carrel in a Philadelphia ad agency to a roomy office next door to Jay Leno's at NBC headquarters. From hobnobbing with the likes of —well—me, to working with big stars, famous politicians, world-class musicians, day after day after day.

Heady work, that can easily expand one's hat size by a few inches. Unless, like Joe, you're a thoroughly grounded person and married to a sensible, value-centered woman like Justine.

I witnessed it first hand during another California trip.

I was set to perform at an LA synagogue and, naturally, called Joe and Justine in the hope of visiting with them. My only free time was Saturday afternoon which happily coincided with a high school graduation party they were holding for their son. Their lovely home was located in "The Valley," not far from where I was staying.

It was a splendid affair, with the Medeiros' East Coast family and about 75 other guests, many of them staff from *The Tonight Show*, filling their home and surrounding the pool.

Hmmm, I thought. This is the big time, all right. LA LA Land, a fancy party. Just like in the movies.

Justine had worked hard, attending to all the details. The cake was to be the centerpiece of the bountiful refreshments. Only the best for this occasion: Pierre, the caterer, passed along the specifications to his Italian bakers: It was to be a chocolate chip cake, with white icing trimmed in blue and gold, the high school colors. And in the center, the words "Congratulations, Justin."

What arrived in the caterer's truck on the day of the party was a chipless all-chocolate cake, with chocolate frosting, and written on it, in white letters, "Congratulations, Justin." And below that, also written in white letters, the words, "Blue and Gold."

Uh oh.

What we had there was an LA party, an important guest list, and a cake from hell. Anyone who has ever seen a movie or read a gossip magazine about LA people can continue the story: Breathless sobbing interspersed with frenetic screams of outrage, threats to Pierre's very life and limb, not to mention his future livelihood, a demand that his bakers be fired, and the promise of lawsuits to come. That's how the story might have continued in classic Hollywood style.

But it didn't. Sure, Justine was disappointed. Who wouldn't be? But what she did was take a serrated knife and scrape off the words "Blue and Gold," making a swirly design with the frosting. She didn't do it quietly or secretively, either. She actually spent much of the afternoon standing by the cake, showing off her artwork, telling the story of the culinary disaster. And laughing.

Laughing. Justine had fun. She had a choice to make, one of those choices we make day in and day out, one of those spur of the moment decisions about how she'd react, how she'd confront what was, after all, an error, a disappointment, a foul-up. And all of this on one of the most important days in her family's history.

She decided to smile. And to laugh. And not to allow the error to ruin the party or consume her energy. What an impressive example of making a sound choice, of exhibiting healthy priorities, and most of all, of modeling compassionate, balanced behavior in front of impressionable kids, friends and family.

It's a certainty that had that cake been perfect, those who saw the inscription might have admired it momentarily, then forgotten it forever. Yet all these years later, the imperfect decoration and Justine's decision not to rant but to laugh, continues to make me smile at her actions and to appreciate her values.

CHAPTER 12

Mrs. Steinberg's Christmas Tree

QUESTION: WHICH JEWISH holiday most closely parallels Christmas?

Answer: Not Hanukkah.

Sure, Hanukkah and Christmas have a few elements in common: both are winter solstice events, successors to the pagan rites of lighting bonfires in an effort to rekindle the increasingly absent sun (it works, by the way; on December 22, the days start to lengthen). Both make use of plenty of candles, or candle-shaped light bulbs. Both involve gift exchanges, though Hanukkah is a latecomer to this tradition.

But it's Passover, not Hanukkah that offers the most similarities to Christmas. Passover: a holiday of special food, remarkable smells, family-centered traditions and memories heaped upon memories. Passover is the Jewish homecoming, the ingathering, based on a historical and theological event upon which the religion was constructed.

Like Christmas.

Always an adaptable, creative people, Jews of the last two generations have invigorated little, rather unimportant Hanukkah (it's not even mentioned in the Hebrew Bible) until it's become nearly competitive with cousin Christmas. What has always been a minor Jewish holiday has been injected with steroids.

And in the myth department, Jews have gone even one step further: while Christian children realize by age six or so (earlier, if they have a cynical older sibling) that Santa is a fable, many Jews actually go through their entire lives thinking that the so-called "miracle" of the oil lamp was a historical and theological event. (It wasn't. The story was simply a cute legend, added hundreds of years after the Maccabean revolt. Sorry if your fantasy has been crushed.)

For Jewish kids, especially Jewish kids like me in the early 1950s, December was a tough month, our feeble little holiday contrasting flimsily against our Christian friends' major joyfest. I even have a vague memory of making an advent wreath in one public school classroom. Every day for several weeks, each of us pulled off one paper ring, watching the wreath grow smaller and smaller, until at the very end, it would be CHRISTMAS! Hooray!! (Oh, except for you, Bobby.)

Back then our family rented a second floor flat on Luzon Avenue in Providence, Rhode Island, just across the street from the John Howland Elementary School. I was in first grade, my sister in third. The flat below was occupied by the landlord and landlady, Mr. and Mrs. Steinberg.

My mother was what we now call a "stay-at-home mom," although in the early fifties, they were called housewives. Friendly and gregarious, she always had a full social life and a huge number of friends. Except for Mrs. Steinberg. Mom and the landlady didn't hit it off very well, possibly because, from the day we moved in, the woman downstairs repeatedly slammed a broomstick into her ceiling every time my sister or I dared walk down our uncarpeted hallway wearing anything more than socks.

Some neighbor.

Within a few months, we moved to another home, but before we could depart, Mrs. Steinberg launched one more missile at our family.

Friday, December 22, 1950. Hanukkah had ended, and Christmas was now right around the corner. School vacation began mid-day, soon after the traditional morning Christmas assembly. Hundreds of excited children bearing holiday artwork streamed through John Howland's doors, followed shortly afterward by their grateful teachers.

My mother had a weekly appointment at the beauty parlor every Friday afternoon. Hair and nails had to be just right, in preparation for the approaching Sabbath. Our teenage babysitter, also beginning vacation, was enlisted to watch us for the two hours. A typical gloomy New England winter day, we played indoors.

The boredom was broken when, shortly after my mother departed, an unexpected peal of the door chimes summoned the three of us down the stairs and into the front hallway. Through the glass, we could see our neighbor, Mrs. Steinberg, patiently waiting. A benign half smile across her lips, she juggled a small box and—my heart began to beat faster—a three-foot-tall, green … Christmas tree!

"A special treat for Margie and Bobby," she explained. Mrs. Steinberg worked as a teacher at an elementary school across town, and the small tree had decorated her room. Her own children were adults, no longer living at home and, well, she knew how much the Alper children must want a Christmas tree.

"And since this perfectly good tree would only have been thrown away, I thought you'd like to have it."

If MasterCard had been around then, they could have produced this ad: A desk-size Douglas fir Christmas tree: $5.50. A small box of ornaments: $2.75. The chance to wreak havoc with the religious identity of the children of your despised neighbor: Priceless.

We accepted the items with thanks and raced up the stairs. But rather than let us set up the tree and begin decorating it, the babysitter, a smart teen, insisted that we first receive parental permission. We dialed the beauty salon and caught my mother with wet hair. "Guess what! We got a Christmas tree! We got a Christmas tree! Mrs. Steinberg gave it to us! We can keep it, right mommy? Just this year, OK? This once?"

Mom was noncommittal on the phone while she furiously rummaged through her pocketbook in a frantic search for Chooz, the antacid gum she favored.

"Don't do anything yet. We'll talk about it when I get home." Mom had bought an hour's reprieve.

We waited impatiently, staring longingly at the naked tree and imagining how enchanting it would look, set on the coffee table in the center of our living room, adorned with decorations. It didn't even occur to us that there were no electric lights. We just wanted a Christmas tree.

During those same moments, as she sat under the sacred privacy of the salon's hair dryer, my mother began to picture what would occur later that evening at our synagogue when she, president of the Sisterhood, and my father, past-president of the Brotherhood, entered services with their children excitedly blabbing the news about their lovely little Christmas tree.

She devised a plan.

A major commotion erupted when Mom returned, with the word "Pleeeeeze" repeated with urgent frequency. Kids' body language appears similar whether they want something really badly or they require an immediate trip to the bathroom: a kind of low jumping, up and down, in place. And my sister and I were jumping. "Please? Can we keep it? Just this once?"

My mother seemed to be considering our request, then launched her counteroffensive. No question about it: she blindsided us with an absolutely perfect, even delicious, solution.

"It is a lovely little tree," she began, "and it was so nice of Mrs. Steinberg to bring it to us." (I now realize that, had my mother been of an earlier, more superstitious background, after saying that sentence she would have automatically spit three times and recited a Yiddish curse. But, third generation American that she was, all she could muster was a veiled, ironic tone, which my sister and I, in our excitement, missed.)

"But you know," she continued, "Christmas isn't our holiday. We have Hanukkah and Passover and Purim. I read in yesterday's *Providence Journal* that there are some children, Christian children here in Providence, who are so poor that they won't even have a Christmas tree for their holiday.

"So, why don't we do this: let's decorate this tree, make it look especially nice, and then, let's phone the police department and ask if they'll give it to some poor children who don't have a tree of their own?"

Touchdown. Bullseye. And grand slam. Mom scored a big one. With her clever proposition, she not only distracted us from begging to keep the tree, but diverted our focus to the point where we simply couldn't wait to get it out of our house and on its way to other children.

Mom placed a call, while my sister and I went to work hanging Mrs. Steinberg's ornaments on the tree, adding some of our own small objects, and gathering toys and books and games to accompany the donation. About an hour later, two very large Providence policemen, wearing their black leather jackets, with guns and nightsticks and handcuffs hanging from their belts, lumbered up the stairs. They spoke briefly with my mother and her wide-eyed children, offered some kind words of gratitude, and then departed, carrying one large bag of stuffed toys along with some boxes of other gifts. And a three-foot tall, artfully decorated Douglas fir Christmas tree.

That scene remains one of the happiest memories of my childhood.

CHAPTER 13

Listening

FOR ME, IT was very much a homecoming, laced with nostalgia, mixed with anxiety.

Let me explain.

During one of my infrequent visits to Philadelphia, where we lived for twelve years, I went off to my old hang-out, The Comedy Cabaret in Doylestown, to do a guest performance.

I hadn't been to the club in ages, so as I entered, there was that flood of memories of a very significant life experience that envelops all of us when we revisit a childhood home, a college campus, a workplace from earlier days. That, as well as the nervousness that attends any comedian going up before an unpredictable audience.

The club is located in a large room above Poco's, a Mexican restaurant. I climbed the familiar stairs, looking at the headshots of the multitude of comedians who'd performed in the room over the decades. When I entered, there was Pete, a physically intimidating gentle giant, still the manager after all these years, sitting by the door as the waitstaff prepared the tables. The stage looked the same: bright lights, red club logo on the wall, one microphone on a pole, one stool.

After chatting with Pete, I began walking to the green room where the comedians gather. As I passed the bar, there was Lisa, Pete's wife. She, too, had been a fixture all these years, tending bar and arranging food. Her back was to me as she collected some glasses.

When she turned, before the warm greeting we gave one another, I saw it. There, pinned to her white shirt was a small black *k'riah* ribbon, the symbol of mourning worn for 30 days by Jews who have lost a parent, a sibling, a child, or a spouse.

I expressed my condolences, and asked what had happened.

Briefly, she told me her father had died a couple of weeks earlier. Her face and her body language radiated sorrow and exhaustion, a sharp and poignant contrast to the anticipated night of laughter the room always provided.

Her main concern was the *k'riah* ribbon. When should it be removed, and what does one then do with it? The comedian passing through the club to do his set became the rabbi for a few moments.

We talked for a short time. Lisa had a lot of setting up to do, and the patrons had begun to arrive.

The show went well.

The ninety minutes of high-spirited laughter and applause sped by, and at the end, the audience slowly departed, the sound level becoming lower and lower. Finally, once again, an empty room. One of the other comics and I hung around, talking comedian talk, exchanging business cards. Comedians form a unique fraternity.

It was late. My colleague had a long drive home and headed out.

The waitstaff had gone, and Pete had walked downstairs to order a late meal. Only Lisa and I remained.

We talked. Or, more accurately, Lisa talked as she closed up the bar.

She told me that her father had died after an automobile accident. He was 85, her mother 83. She has three siblings, but Lisa is the one closest to her mom.

She shared details of her father's death, and how draining and complex it had been. She guided her mother through mourning, somehow managing the pieces of the elderly woman's radically changed life even as she herself was devastated by her dad's sudden passing.

A few more moments passed, then a brief hug. I headed out the door, and started walking down the stairs.

Half-way, I heard Lisa's voice again and looked up. She stuck her head around the corner from inside the club, and said, simply, "Thank you for listening."

That was all. I continued on my way, waved to Pete, sitting at a table, and walked out into the night.

~

Every one of us who has lost loved ones is part of a huge support group, if we care to recognize it.

"Thanks for listening." A reminder of what we need to do to comfort mourners, and what we need to find in order to receive comfort ourselves.

We need to listen carefully, with empathy, with compassion, with sorrow, sometimes with tears, to the words—even the most mundane words—of those who mourn, those who are suffering.

And whenever we mourn, like Lisa, in the immediate wake of a death or, like most of us, on normal days and at times when memories and pain flow, we need to find patient listeners who will gently hear our stories when we so need to tell them.

Even in the most unlikely settings. A comedy club, for example, with caricatures of Bill Cosby and The Three Stooges silently smiling in the background.

When two people listen patiently to each other, God listens to them too.

—Talmud

CHAPTER **14**

The Orphan

I ATE LUNCH there at least once a week, sometimes twice.

Definitely not because of the décor. The place seated about 30, maybe 40 if you include the counter against one of the walls and the two small tables out on the porch which could be used on more balmy days. The chairs were yard-sale rejects, some with tufts of stuffing emerging from under the plastic seat covers, others with spindles missing and way, way out of balance. Or perhaps it was the uneven floor that made them tilt.

The walls were usually covered with paintings and drawings, products of the "talented" young adult offspring of regular patrons. The works ran the gamut from the occasionally lovely to schlock, depressing, and generally unappetizing, but there they hung, unsold, but truthfully generating an honest line in a budding artist's resume: Exhibited at "The Village Fare, Manchester, Vermont."

"The Village Fare." Kind of a Renaissance-sounding name, although the place was anything but. It was eclectic, occupying a creaky old building that in my years in Manchester has seen six or seven incarnations, from grocery to souvenirs store, to coffee house and restaurant, serving breakfast and lunch, but never on Mondays.

I loved the place. It closed a few years back, and nothing in town has come near to replacing it.

First of all, the food was usually terrific, although once I nearly broke my teeth on an unusually crusty piece of bread. Another time I considered calling in the volunteer fire department after chowing down some particularly spicy chili. Paula, who did most of the cooking, warned me on that one. The dishes all bore creative names, such as the Humble Bumble and Italian Rascal sandwiches, and Chilly Dilly cucumber soup.

You ordered your meal through the kitchen window in the back, they took your name, and a few minutes later someone would wander out, calling "Herb?" Most of the staff knew me, but when there was somebody new working the window and they asked my name, I usually replied, with a straight face, "Ummm. It's Steve Martin. But just call out 'Bob.'"

The Village Fare also provided a nice blend of locals and tourists, and since I work at home, alone each day, the chance to schmooze with familiar and unfamiliar faces offered an enticing mid-day break. Occasionally a celebrity dropped in: the Village Fare was Tom Snyder's favorite Vermont eating establishment.

But the primary reason I frequented the restaurant was Ken Farrell, the co-owner, along with Paula Sweeney. Ken baked bread in the cellar and drove the delivery van, but his favorite role was working the counter, where he doled out pastry and cappuccino, ran the cash register, and kibitzed with the customers. And could he ever kibitz!

Ken's about my age. In the course of his life he's been an actor, a housepainter, a voice-over artist, a roofer, and years ago, he was in the original cast of *The Proposition*, a comedy improv group. Ken did great imitations of bewildered tourists from New York or New Jersey or Connecticut, and he thoroughly enjoyed getting to know all the folks who wandered into his domain. He often asked, "So, where are you from?" which led to friendly conversations and, not unexpectedly, lots of repeat business.

That's the main reason I visited The Village Fare: Ken. It's like the late Harry Golden's story about his father, an avowed atheist who attended synagogue daily.

"Why do you go to *shul*," he asked his father, "if you don't believe in God?"

To which the elderly man answered, "Each person goes to synagogue for a different reason. Garfinkle goes to talk to God. I go to talk to Garfinkle."

As for The Village Fare, I went to talk to Ken.

When The Village Fare was quiet, when the tourists were safely back in New York or New Jersey or Connecticut, during weeks after foliage had ended, or during the post-winter period we call Mud Season, Ken often shared with me gleanings from recent encounters. One year, when the large Equinox Resort Hotel across the street was made thoroughly kosher and filled with ultra-Orthodox Jews for the days of Passover, Ken reported that two of the guests would go for a jog some mornings, sneaking into his place at the end of their run for forbidden sweet rolls.

Jokes, stories, quips, funky music … they were all part of The Village Fare mix. It's what I expected, and generally found.

But one day, something different happened. It was during the quiet Mud Season, and even though I arrived at one o'clock, usually the height of the mid-day rush, only a couple of tables were occupied by local people I knew. Paula and one helper were just killing time back in the kitchen.

Ken stood behind the counter, tidying up some displays and restocking the small salad bar that sits just to the right of the cash register.

When Ken and I chatted, he didn't ask, "Where are you from?" With me, it was "Where are you going?" at which point I'd fill him in on my comedy schedule.

"Orlando, Chicago, Los Angeles. But," I joked, "best of all, I just booked Scranton, Pennsylvania, for June."

Ken put down the spoon and dish he was holding.

"Scranton," he said. "Scranton." Looking more serious than I can ever remember him, he told me that just the previous week, two elderly nuns, passing through Vermont, had come into The Village Fare for lunch. As usual, Ken engaged them in conversation, particularly since Ken himself had been born a Catholic and attended parochial school for years and years.

"Where you from?" he asked them.

"Scranton," one nun answered. "We served at the Saint Joseph Home, an orphanage."

Ken felt the wind leave his lungs, and then recovered. "Saint Joseph," he said. "That's where I spent the first two years of my life."

Ken had been an orphan. An orphan in the old days, not so very long ago, when such unfortunate children spent months, years, even their entire childhoods in institutions, rather than foster care as is done routinely today.

So there he stood, behind his counter in his funky Village Fare restaurant, on a gloomy late winter day chatting with two retired nuns passing through Vermont. On the wall above Ken's head, some colorful signs he had constructed promoted Turkey Lurkey sandwich specials and offered four varieties of what he branded "Trendy Coffee."

Bread dough, rolled into loaves, coated with flour and ready for the oven, rested on a low shelf, while an antique cash register, now silent, awaited the next customer.

"Yes, Saint Joseph," one nun repeated. "It's closed now, but of course, years ago, it was the biggest orphanage in the area."

The nuns smiled. The conversation grew lively.

"When did it close?" Ken asked. "How many children went through there?"

Small details. Nothing earth-shaking.

And then they compared dates: Ken's month and year of birth, the nuns' dates of service at the orphanage.

They coincided. The nuns worked there when Ken, an infant, arrived.

And that's when it happened. One of the nuns thought for a moment, nodded her head conclusively, looked straight at Ken and said, simply, softly, with a sort of knowing, satisfied smile, "Why, then, I held you."

At which point Ken Farrell, the kibitzer, the restaurant host, gregarious, animated, outgoing, funny—Ken Farrell lowered his head.

And began to weep.

CHAPTER 15

Thanks.
I Needed That.

What soap is to the body, laughter is to the soul.
—Yiddish proverb

LATE MORNING. A fairly quiet time at the Atlanta Airport.

I was flying home, and though I already had my boarding pass and didn't need to check luggage, I decided to stop by the USAirways counter to see if I could charm my way into an upgrade or at least a more comfortable exit row seat.

By my quick calculation, it had been about two years since I'd passed through Hartsfield, so it was even more surprising when, as I approached the agent, she looked across the desk and said, "You're Mr. Alper, right?"

Maybe she remembered me because of my engaging personality or exceptional good looks.

Or, perhaps, she remembered me because of my driver's license, which looks like this:

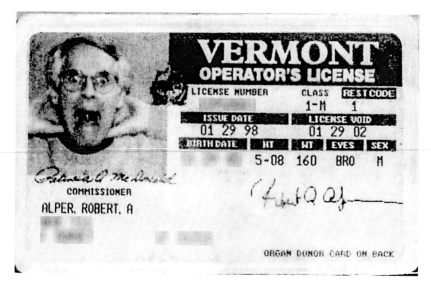

I suppose this is not exactly what one would expect when examining the ID of Rabbi Dr. Robert A. Alper, B.A., B.H.L., M.A.H.L, D.D., D.Min., but then again, comedy is all about surprising people with the unexpected, and this license has always been my most effective prop.

It's real. About 60 percent of the people who see it eventually exclaim, "They let you do that?" At which point I instruct them to turn the license over, where they see:

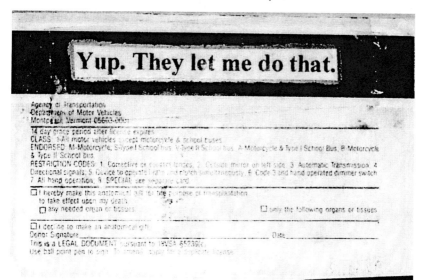

They did let me do that. Twice. Vermonters are a bit more relaxed than most Americans, and the hustle and bustle and long lines that characterize motor vehicle bureaus in metropolitan areas find no parallels in our mostly rural state. So when it came time to snap my photo, I asked about the regulations.

"No hats."

"Fine."

The Department of Motor Vehicles clerk was in a good mood, and apparently secure in her job, because after she realized what I was up to, she actually suggested a way to refine my pose. Four years later, I left the small building with a similar photo on my license. But on the third go-round, a grinch had assumed command of the office, and the timid young photographer thought it best to check with his superior before snapping the shutter. When I saw the boss stroll out of the back office, I knew my days of possessing a unique license had ended. At least for four years.

I still carry the old license, and share it as often as possible.

To be honest, the act of amusing people serves my ego. Any response, from a chuckle to a guffaw, is validation, affirmation, applause. That in itself might be enough but, like so many elements of comedy the use of this driver's license "prop" has had heartwarming, unanticipated results that go far beyond a quick smile or laugh.

Another airport, another license story.

This time it was Detroit, on one of those cold, gray, dreary mornings in early winter. I picked up my rental car and drove to one of the booths at the lot's exit. Since I rent cars often, I know the routine: pull up to the window, hand over the rental document and my driver's license.

"Yes, I see that the tank is full."

"No, thanks, I'll decline the refuel option."

"Have a nice day."

As is often the case, the person working in the booth was a foreigner, a thin, dark man with an accent I guessed to be

Pakistani. He greeted me with a proper, somewhat blank expression, just doing his job, as he did eight hours every day, checking documents against the numbers on the dashboards and in his computer. Over and over and over, car after car after car.

Except when he looked at my license. First, he checked the expiration date, and made sure that the auto's ID number matched his records. And finally, he glanced at the photo. Then he took a second look. And for the first time, he smiled. A broad, joyous smile, complemented by uplifted eyebrows, slightly confused eyes and a quiet laugh.

"This license real?" I assured him it was proper, and he examined it more closely.

"Do you mind," he asked, "I show this to friend in next booth?" I sat there watching across the neighboring lane as two men with truly boring, repetitive jobs took a moment out to examine my photo.

When he returned to his station, the man's blank appearance had been replaced by a warm grin.

"You made my day," he told me.

And his smile made my day.

It's almost predictable how people react to that driver's license. Unless the viewer is angry, ultra-busy or terribly depressed, the response is a lightened mood, a smile, a laugh. But it's more than that. Sharing humor tears down interpersonal barriers and jump-starts a more intimate relationship. Some of the benefits are highly spiritual. Others, very practical.

I landed at Newark Airport just as a major snowstorm started to blanket the area. I had reserved a mid-size car, and now dreaded driving back and forth to somewhere in the middle of New Jersey on slippery roads. So before I handed over my license, I asked a strange question. "If I make you smile, will you give me a car that'll be good in snow?" The agent didn't quite understand, until she saw the photo. A few minutes later, I left the lot in a nearly new, all-wheel-drive Jeep equipped with four snow tires.

The same thing happens in hotels. Always said with a very straight face, my trademark "If I make you laugh, will you consider giving me an upgrade?" is frequently rewarded by a room on the concierge level. Other times, it's placement in a newly refurbished mini-suite, or a better view, or a complimentary breakfast. People like to be amused, they welcome an interjection of unexpected humor into their routine, and they often respond generously. After looking at my license and the usual back-and-forth about the photo, one hotel clerk put it this way: "Man, it's been a tough night here. Thanks. I needed that!"

～

I imagine that I inherited some kind of genetic predisposition toward humor. My maternal grandfather was a very funny man. I remember how, when I was about seven, Grandpa Edgar would relax in his overstuffed easy chair, large cigar clenched firmly between his teeth. He'd call me over to him, and as I approached he'd reach ever so slowly into his pocket and pull out his wallet. He'd rustle through it, and then recite deliberately, feigning dead earnest, "Bobby. I'm going to let you look … at a FIVE DOLLAR BILL."

He'd show it to me, then reinsert it into his wallet, which he'd place back in his pocket.

We both thought it was a pretty funny bit and, of course, eventually Grandpa would turn the money over to me for being such a good partner in his game.

My father, too, had a decent sense of humor, though for him long, very long stories were the standard, which is probably why I gravitated toward the quick-hit style of stand-up comedy. Dad also had an appreciation of the absurd, and a knack for amusing unsuspecting people he'd encounter.

For much of his life, he was a traveling salesman, driving throughout the east, staying in hotels and motels, passing the non-working hours alone or with strangers. Like waitresses. His favorite story is one which, when I think about it, parallels my own driver's license tale: a moment in which a serious-looking customer produces something out of far left field, completely reframing the encounter.

As Dad related, he was somewhere in northern Maine, calling on a client at a large paper mill. It was a modest little town, with one hotel, one pharmacy, and a few specialty stores. In the evening, there was nothing to do but complete his paperwork and walk over to the only restaurant for a late dinner.

By 8:30 the place had all but emptied out. Only my father, the unseen cook in the back, and a weary, matronly waitress remained. Dad had eaten his main course, and was now slowly finishing the diner's signature item, homemade apple pie. The waitress was not impatient. She had chores to do before they could close: fill the salt and sugar dispensers, wash down the tables and counter, start the sweeping. But it was obvious that she was exhausted after a long day on her feet.

At one point she passed near my father, and with a kindly smile asked this visitor, alone, far from home, "How's the pie?"

My father nodded thoughtfully, swallowed the bite that was in his mouth, and with a slight, nostalgic sigh replied, "You know, this pie is just like my mother used to make."

The waitress was moved. "Oh, that's so sweet."

"Yes," Dad continued. "It's undercooked, soggy, and flavorless. My mother couldn't bake to save her life."

The waitress laughed so hard, she nearly dropped the tray of catsup bottles she was holding.

Out of the unexpected, laughter. For this woman, a fine end to a hard day.

(My grandmother, by the way, was actually a spectacular baker. With a good sense of humor. She loved hearing my father tell this story.)

∼

There are millions of ways to evoke laughter and smiles in our day-to-day interactions. One way is to "be a clown," as the old Cole Porter song recommends:

Be a clown, be a clown,
All the world loves a clown.
Act a fool, play the calf,
And you'll always have the last laugh.
Wear the cap and the bells
And you'll rate with all the great swells

With the exception of telling jokes, being a clown is not quite my style, even though I'd really like to "rate with all the great swells." I prefer that quiet, sober, unexpected method, delivering humor masked by a straight face with no warning as to the real intention of my words. It's somewhat of an art form, and it provides me, and often the listeners, with welcome amusement.

Thus, for amateur readers, it's my pleasure to present:

Rabbi Bob Alper's Practical Guide to Evoking Laughter in Mundane Situations, Utilizing True Examples from Real Life.

* Here's an easy one, but it's predicated on your driving without an automatic toll payment device like E-Z Pass affixed to your windshield. If the toll is $2, for example, and I have two dollar bills handy, I look at the collector while handing over the money and ask, "Do you accept exact change?"

There's usually a moment of silence here as thoughts churn in the collector's head. Some of the time I get a quizzical look and a simple—and I mean very simple—"Yes." Other times, however, the recipient gets the joke and we engage in quick, pleasant back and forth before the driver in the car behind me begins leaning on the horn.

I often pull the "do you accept exact change" routine in over-the-counter commercial transactions, and have noticed that adults understand the concept, but it almost invariably passes directly over the heads of teenagers. I've even stood by, amazed, as some of the kids actually left their posts to consult with their supervisor as to whether they can "accept exact change." It's at those moments that I really begin to worry about our nation's future. As I did on another occasion, when I purchased a comb, asked the teen clerk, "Does this come with instructions?" and received only a depressingly blank stare.

✳ And there's yet another arrow in my humor quiver that the teens never seem to appreciate, while adults almost always do. When the person at the cash register says, "Your total is eighteen forty-five," I'll affect a quick look of amazement and reply: "What a coincidence! That's the year my mother was born!"

✳ At many of the large chain restaurants, if there's a wait for a table, the host or hostess will ask for your name, which they then shout out once your table is ready. Occasionally, I'll reply to the name request with a lowered voice and ultra-serious expression: "I'm not allowed to tell you. I'm in the Witness Protection Program." Other times, I'll politely but firmly insist, "Please call me 'Your Royal Highness.'" It's a thrill to see how heads turn when patrons hear, "Your Royal Highness, table for four."

✳ I frequently eat lunch in local places that take your order at the counter and then deliver the food to your table. One afternoon I was alone, about to pay for my selection, when the clerk looked over my shoulder to see a woman of about 85 standing in line behind me. Before taking my money, she asked, "Are you two together?" I glanced at the elderly woman, pretended to mull things over for a moment, and replied with a subtle leer, "Not yet."

My words went right over the clerk's head. No acknowledgement whatsoever. But the lady behind me definitely enjoyed the joke. A few minutes later, as I passed the small table where she had sat down, she looked up at me and shot me an adorable conspiratorial grin.

✳ Parents of little kids love this one: When I see a two-year-old, for example, running around, giggling, dancing, with her exhausted-looking parents standing by, trying to juggle strollers and baby bags and, perhaps, another child or two, I approach them, unsmiling, looking almost critical, and say, "You should try to get this kid to cheer up."

* For our dog, Barney, a mid-size rescue "mongrelian" originally from Puerto Rico, every day is a tricks-for-treats variant on Halloween. He accompanies me to the post office, the bank, and the pharmacy, where he collects his goodies and everyone greets him by name. Then they occasionally acknowledge me as well. When I use the bank's drive-through window, the receipt comes back to me in the drawer, along with a dog biscuit. I usually smile at the teller, and say, "Thanks! May I have one for Barney, too?"

* There's no immediate feedback from creatively playing with internet forms, but I suspect that somewhere out in the world in a merchandise fulfillment center or in a billing office or at the UPS transfer station, the fake company name I usually use, "Chickenlips Productions," draws a chuckle or two. And when a snoopy form asks for my "position" in my company, without fail I enter the word "king." When the form asks for income, I always write, "YES."

* Telemarketers are a class unto themselves. Basically, I feel compassion for folks in this line of work, except for the thieves who use their phones to prey on the elderly and naïve. But most are just doing their job, usually reading from prepared scripts, some of which direct them to ask intrusive questions. Here's how I handle those encounters:

Me: "I want to cancel this credit card."

Telemarketer: "May I ask WHY you want to cancel?"

Me: "Umm. I just don't need it."

Telemarketer: "WHY? Don't you want to receive airline miles with purchases?"

Me: "No, I've got too many cards."

Telemarketer: "How about if we waive the annual fee?"

Me: "Nope. Look, I guess I need to be totally upfront with you: I'm cancelling because every time I touch this card, I get gassy."

That pretty much ends the negotiations. At this point the telemarketer usually departs from the script, and we share a laugh as he punches in the information that will terminate my relationship with his company. He's lost a customer, but he's happy.

✳ Our home answering machine provides me with an unlimited opportunity to experiment with new material. Years ago, when our kids still resided with us, the outgoing message consisted of my voice only, announcing, "You've reached the Alper family. I'm Bob! I'm Sherri! I'm Zack! And I'm Jessie! We all sound alike, because we've been living together for a long time." Later, I changed the message to "This is the Alper home. Please speak in a clear, distinct voice, but not so loud that you wake the dog. And, uh, don't mumble, like you usually do."

And one of my all-time favorites: "You've reached 555-4337. As of next month, our number will be re-hyphenated, becoming 5554-337. Please make a note of it." I can still hear, with a smile, the very first response. "He-lo-oh. It's your mother. I don't get it!"

✳ There's no end to airplane jokes and routines, probably because professional comedians spend lots of time above the clouds, with few distractions and plenty of opportunity to conjure up new material. My favorite is to watch the flight attendant as he or she works the beverage cart down the aisle. If they look stern, or harassed, or rushed, I simply place my order and go back to watching the movie on my laptop. But if the attendant seems pleasant, and chatty, which most do, I silently prepare.

Eventually, eye contact is established with me, the white-haired businessman-looking guy sitting in 15D.

"What will you have to drink?" to which I reply, with the most serious of expressions, "I'd like *either* a tall, low-fat, decaf latte. Or Coke." It usually gets a decent reaction, often with the attendant adding, "Hey, I could go for one of those myself!" (This interchange reminds me of the old joke about the El Al flight attendant who asks a passenger if he'd like dinner. "Sure," the man says. "What are my choices?" To which the flight attendant responds, "Yes. And no.")

⁎ And finally, in light of the nature of the things I do and say when out and about, I printed a set of cards, adapted from those designed by one of my cleverest colleagues, and gave them to my wife. She was amused, but reticent, so I share them myself with people I encounter day to day.

Mrs. Robert A. Alper

wishes to apologize
for her husband's behavior

on the morning of _____

on the afternoon of _____

on the evening of _____

Making people laugh as a passion and as a profession garners a host of rewarding dividends. But none more fascinating than this email, which I share in its entirety:

> Hello,
>
> I'm not sure if this is actually Bob Alper's You-Tube account or someone who simply admires his work.
>
> Rabbi, if this is you, I just want to say thank you. I listen to the satellite radio every day on the way to work. I work in a maximum-security correctional facility and I get to work with some really "interesting" people with some special personality quirks. Fortunately on the way in and on the

way out I am able to listen to the comedy channels and I always get to chuckle when I hear you.

Thanks for helping me stay mellow enough not to strangle someone to death.

～

Among those I like or admire, I can find no common denominator, but among those whom I love, I can: all of them make me laugh.

—W.H. Auden.

CHAPTER **16**

Growing Old with a Smile

SOMEHOW THE TWO of us ended up walking out of the Bennington Free Library at the same moment. I had either given a lecture of some sort, or participated in a panel. I don't recall exactly, since it took place quite a while ago.

Rose introduced herself, and we stood on the sidewalk chatting, enjoying the quiet Vermont summer evening. She was short, wizened, probably in her mid-eighties, and intellectually sharp as a tack. At first, she shared with me memories of my parents, whom she knew when they had lived in Bennington three decades earlier. And then, as often happens when people find themselves in conversation with a rabbi, a question.

Despite my earlier suggestion that she call me Bob, Rose adopted a more formal mode. "I have a problem, rabbi," she began. "I feel terrible. Last week, I went to the liquor store to buy my monthly fifth of vodka. While I was there, I lost a money clip that had been given to my son at his bar mitzvah more than fifty years ago.

"I guess," she said with a resigned look, "God is telling me, 'No more booze.'"

The latter statement was offered with a slight twinkle, but also some real distress at the thought, maybe divinely ordered, that she surrender yet another pleasurable element of her life, an occasional cocktail with friends.

I decided to challenge her theological conclusion, and to do so in the way I knew best. "Yeah, maybe that's what God was telling you. But on the other hand, maybe God was saying, 'Rose. Get a wallet!'"

We shared a good laugh, and from that time forward, whenever I encountered Rose, she reminded, me, with a lovely grin, of our theological discussion. She never recovered her money clip. But she continued to treat herself to her monthly fifth of vodka.

I'm glad that the accident of our departure from the library at the same moment resulted in the conversation Rose and I had. I would hate to think that the loss of a money clip might lead, through a naïve theological leap, to the loss of one of the few diminishing pleasures left to an elderly woman.

"Grow old along with me! The best is yet to be ..." Robert Browning wrote. Well, not necessarily. Especially when one understands that much of growing old involves loss. Loss of cherished companions, loss of physical powers, loss of dreams, loss of self-confidence. And loss of independence.

I suspect that underlying Rose's decision to share the money clip story with an accidentally available rabbi reflected her distress over yet another sign that her own strength, her ability to organize her personal affairs, was being eclipsed by forgetfulness and carelessness.

For my parents, as for many elderly persons, one of the clearest symbols of that process of loss centered on the ability to drive an automobile safely.

My father, six years older than my mother, was the first to reach that unenviable stage in life. In his mid-seventies, he occasionally dozed off for a few seconds at stoplights, and then, within a period of a few months, misjudged distances and scraped alongside other cars when maneuvering through narrow streets.

Our family was fortunate. With little urging, Dad sold his car and stopped driving. In other families, the same process can become a wrenching, nightmarish power struggle, sometimes only resolved with the enlistment of physicians, lawyers, and even police. Or it can result in a tragedy.

I wish I had been more understanding, more empathic about what Dad must have been feeling at that time in his life. I wish I had been more gracious. I wish I had told him that I was proud of him, much like when he, as a young father, had told me he was proud of me when I took my own major steps.

Fifteen years later, and after 12 years as a very independent widow, my 80-year-old mother called.

"That's it. No more driving. I've decided to quit." Clear and direct. Mom had been involved in a couple of close calls, and recognizing that she had reached one of life's crossroads, she made a difficult choice wisely and with grace.

This time I responded appropriately, with compassion, congratulating her on her decision. But more than that, I began to think that, just like a graduation or a retirement, the voluntary discontinuance of driving is an event that might be better endured through a celebration. I began to imagine a wholly new life cycle event that recognizes a difficult, intelligent choice and a major change in a lifestyle.

A ceremony like this:

The setting: Curbside.

Participants: Allyne Alper, a congregation of her family and friends, and an officiant, who could be either a rabbi (must be licensed) or, in the absence of a spiritual leader, an authorized representative of the Department of Motor Vehicles.

OFFICIANT: Allyne, as you face your white 1992 Buick Skylark with blue velvet interior and only 19,541 original miles, I ask: Do you of your own free will and consent hereby surrender your driver's license and promise to refrain from driving?

ALLYNE: I do.

CONGREGATION: (sighs of relief).

OFFICIANT: And do you, Allyne's family and friends, promise, to the best of your ability, to transport Allyne to various destinations, in fair weather and in foul, in heat and in cold, in daylight or even at night?

CONGREGATION: We do. Except for those of us who don't like to drive at night.

ALLYNE: Irma, you and Fred can take me to symphony. I already have a ride to mah jong, and the bridge game is in the apartment next to mine. Debby and David and the children said they'd bring me to temple next Friday and ….

OFFICIANT: Excuse me. We need to continue. By the authority vested in me by the Department of Motor Vehicles, and with the consent of these witnesses, I hereby pronounce you "non-driver." We shall now cut your license in two.

ALLYNE: Feh, it was a terrible photo anyway. I'd much rather use my passport.

OFFICIANT: Allyne, to confirm your new status and celebrate this sacred transition in your life, I joyously invite you to assume your place of honor in the passenger seat.

At this point, windshield washer fluid is squirted festively into the air. In addition, persons of Sephardic background may wish to stroke the car with a chamois cloth, as is their custom.

The horn is sounded.

∽

It was too late to arrange such an event for Mom, but she loved seeing the written ceremony I devised, and she took great personal joy in knowing that it was constructed with her in mind.

And yes, she thought it was pretty funny, too.

CHAPTER 17

It Only Hurts When You Laugh

"IT ONLY HURTS when you laugh."

And when you cough, I might add.

Not the first cough. That wasn't painful at all. It's what took place a few weeks later that really caught my attention.

The spring of 1972 was a pretty delicious time in my life. I was finishing up my final year of rabbinical seminary in Cincinnati, had been hired for my first pulpit, and could therefore count the weeks before saying farewell to the grad student years of "genteel poverty." But most important, in an absolutely splendid example of planned parenthood, Sherri was due to give birth to our first child a week before my ordination.

My thesis had been accepted and I had only a modest class schedule, so we spent our days preparing for our child and for our move to Buffalo. With time on my hands, I decided to take advantage of the school's decent health plan, and undergo a routine physical with the kindly internist who oversaw the health of generations of young rabbis.

"Cough," he directed. I obliged.

"Hmmm. You have a double hernia."

That diagnosis came as a total surprise. The doctor suggested, and I agreed, that since I had an empty schedule between early June's ordination and the mid-July move to Buffalo, it would be a good time to have the surgery.

Zack was born on May 28th, he and Sherri came home four days later, and on June 2nd, Sherri sat with my family, watching as I was ordained. One of my classmates, unsuccessfully masking his self-righteousness, asked how we could leave our week-old infant with a sitter. I assured him that the woman we'd engaged had cared for newborns for over forty years, while at that point, Sherri and I had amassed a grand total of two days' experience.

Three weeks later, it was time for my surgery.

These days, hernia repairs are often done on an outpatient basis, but in 1972, mine consisted of a full-scale operation, total anesthesia, with three or four days of hospital recuperation followed by a similar length of home bed rest. The surgery went well, but the first night was not as smooth: hour after hour I had to listen as my roommate, hidden behind a divider curtain, muttered, "Oh, Lordy Lordy, Lordy" with each and every breath.

During one of her visits, Sherri brought an adorable surprise, something to cheer me up. A friend from Arkansas had sent a baby gift, which Sherri carefully removed from the bag. First, a little blue checkered pair of infant pants. I smiled. Then a tiny vest, made of the same material. I grinned.

And finally, a baby hat, in the same blue checkered pattern, a rather rakish, precious, adult-style design. I imagined how funny it would look on our tiny kid, and then, without thinking, I laughed. OW!

Which made me need to cough. OUCH!!

When someone has recently been playing around with the tender, interior parts of your abdomen, it's simply not advisable to laugh. Or cough.

In this case, it was absolutely true: "It only hurts when you laugh."

But we know that, with some exceptions such as hernia surgery, laughter can be a powerful healing device. This is nothing new. Proverbs teaches that "a merry heart does like good medicine." (17:22) while in Ecclesiastes we are told, "A season is set for everything … a time to weep; a time to laugh." (3:1,4) And we're also reminded in that same book that we moderns didn't invent this concept. "There's nothing new under the sun." (1:9)

A rather recent phenomenon, though, is the purposeful introduction of laughter to the art of healing.

Humor, laughter, it turns out, is much more than pleasant diversion. It's much more than entertainment. Laughter is life-giving, life-affirming, and increasing its incorporation into our lives is a splendid way to enhance our physical and spiritual health.

Having a well-developed sense of humor, experts tell us, can be a tremendous asset in meeting day-to-day stress or even major challenges. And the physical ramifications of laughter are well-documented. The classic book, of course, is Norman Cousins' *Anatomy of an Illness* in which the former editor of *The Saturday Review* documented how, while battling a serious disease, he checked himself out of the hospital and into a hotel room equipped with a slew of Marx Bothers and Candid Camera films. As he explained, "I made the joyous discovery that ten minutes of genuine belly laughter had an anesthetic effect and would give me at least two hours of pain-free sleep."

Laughter stimulates the release of endorphins, the body's own pain-fighting enzymes. It's also been proven that laughter can lessen the perception of pain, increase tolerance of discomfort, and raise the heart rate as much as aerobic exercise.

In fact, laughter has been called "internal aerobics," a term describing the host of positive physical benefits that can be garnered from a few strong belly laughs. Unless, of course, the person doing that laughing has had recent surgery for a double hernia.

With the value of humor now firmly verified scientifically, many in the medical establishment are responding creatively, equipping hospitals with humor rooms or humor carts filled with comedy videos, silly costumes, games, and the like.

Dr. Bernie Siegel, a cancer surgeon wrote, "Show me a patient who is able to laugh and play, who enjoys living and I'll show you someone who is going to live longer. Laughter makes the unbearable bearable, and a patient with a well-developed sense of humor has a better chance of recovery than a stolid individual who seldom laughs."

And my pseudo-scientific report on humor and health? One Tuesday morning, the elderly women of the Dorset, Vermont, Congregational Church sewing group played one of my comedy CDs during their weekly session. Afterward, reliable sources told me, one lady declared, "Why, I laughed so hard, I won't even need to use my eye drops this afternoon!"

A cute story. But other reports have been even more meaningful to me. Such as the way a young woman named Beverly endured chemotherapy. Sitting in a room filled with lounge chairs and IV drips, where anxiety permeated the air as the patients spent the hours reading, or thinking, or trying not to think, Beverly hooked up her iPod to a double set of earphones, so that she and her husband could pass the time together laughing at my jokes.

And I remember another young woman who related how, while visiting her parents during an early month of her first pregnancy, she miscarried, and later had to drive back to her home, alone, some four hours distant. She told me that she listened to my CDs for part of the way. The distraction lifted her grim mood, and helped her complete the sad journey. (I should mention that as she was telling this story, we were occasionally interrupted by her two adorable, very energetic, toddlers.)

There are many uplifting examples of the ways that laughter has helped people through painful times. My favorite story is told by my friend Tommy Moore, a professional comedian for nearly 40 years who volunteers as a hospital clown. Tommy explains that when working on the wards, the first rule is always to check with the nurses to determine which patients are appropriate to visit.

"One day," he wrote, "my clown partner and I broke that rule. Printout in hand, we were beckoned into a room that wasn't on the list, by a woman who was obviously the wife of a patient.

"I figured, it was a command performance, so we'll bend the rule. As we walked in, the wife was saying 'Look honey, it's a clown. Open your eyes!' With his eyes now wide open, he barely mustered a smile during our three-minute mini-show."

For a comedian or clown, three minutes like those, trying to make someone laugh and seeming to fail miserably, are, in comedy parlance, like dying. Which is how Tommy and his partner felt, until they started to leave, and the wife took both of their hands and began thanking them profusely.

Surprised, and even confused, Tommy offered, "Well, we really didn't do that much." At which point the wife explained, "You don't understand. This is the first time in months my husband has opened his eyes."

We love successes like these. But a word of caution: it's also important that we not see laughter as a cure-all, and, more significant, that we not see the absence of humor as some kind of weakness or guilt-producing moral failure. Recall what comes before "a time to laugh" in Ecclesiastes: "To every thing there is a season … A time to weep and a time to laugh." Sometimes, with illness, it is simply, and only, a time to weep.

Coping with serious illness does not only involve pain and confrontation with one's mortality. Often, there are additional issues involved, such as helplessness, humiliation, frustration, and anger. My mother experienced all of these during the days leading to her death in a hospital at age 86. Yet, in one situation, humor afforded some welcome respite.

It seemed like a quiet afternoon on the ward. Nobody rushing about, no emergency calls for crash carts and the like. Just a sort of normal day. I was alone with Mom, now very weak and completely bedridden, when she pushed her call button.

Some patients are excessively demanding and entitled. Mom was not. She simply needed help.

"Yes, Mrs. Alper?" a voice crackled through the loudspeaker above her head.

"I need a bed pan."

"OK."

Ten minutes passed. Mom buzzed again, and received assurance that someone would come to her room shortly.

They did not. A few minutes later, my anger rising, I offered to walk out into the hallway and hijack some help. My mother looked up, sadly. "Too late."

I started to rise from my chair, but Mom stopped me. Eternally the people pleaser, she cautioned, "It won't do any good, and I don't want them to be angry with me." Part of the negotiation dance one does when so utterly dependent on the ministrations of strangers.

I then had an idea which I shared with Mom. With her agreement, we decided to wait, to watch the clock to see just how long it would take for help to arrive following her call.

An hour went by.

As those minutes passed, of course, we were both feeling outraged and helpless, and I was particularly upset at the sad irony of the indignity suffered by a woman who, throughout her life, had always been so meticulous and so attentive to the welfare of others. When the 60th minute arrived, it was time for action.

I could have demanded to see the unit supervisor, or lodged a complaint with the hospital CEO, or enlisted help from the hospital's patient advocate, or thrown a bedpan into the large fish tank in the lounge. Instead, I quietly made my way into the main corridor, to the "T" intersection where two hallways meet and the nursing station is centrally located. Three or four nurses and aides sat and stood behind the desk, some working on charts while two were engaged in a conversation, snippets of which included the name of a celebrity who'd been caught in a scandal.

I nodded as I walked past, but said nothing.

When I reached the central point of the hallway, from which one can see to the end of all three corridors, I knelt on the carpet, then lay down on my back, placed my hands under my head, and began to stare at the ceiling.

About 15 seconds later, one of nurses ran up to me. "Sir, are you all right?"

Without changing position, I looked up at her and answered matter-of-factly, "Oh yeah, sure." I went back to staring at the ceiling.

A moment later, a very concerned head nurse rushed over, accompanied by his assistant. "What's happened? Were you dizzy? Did you fall?"

By now I was starting to get up. And as I did, I said, very calmly, "No, I'm fine. I just wanted to get some attention."

I explained what precipitated my hospital theatrics, not with the anger I was still feeling, but in a level tone, a calm description of what my mother was forced to endure followed by my questioning whether this incident was representative of the kind of care she was receiving overall.

To his credit, the head nurse could not have been nicer. Obviously mortified, he asked me for a detailed description of my mother's unanswered calls and wrote a lengthy report, all the while assuring me that he would monitor her future care personally.

I couldn't return to Mom's room for a while; the door was closed, as a pair of aides did what needed to be done. When they departed and I entered, Mom was sitting up in her bed, refreshed, still very ill and weak, but graced with a conspiratorial smile, eager to hear what had taken place at the nurses' station.

She was delighted and amused and, in a way, empowered. For the next few days, until she became too ill to converse easily, she joyfully and proudly told visitors about our creative conspiracy to solve a problem.

And from that point forward, until the night she died, help always came moments after she pressed the call button.

CHAPTER **18**

The Little Grief Counselor

IT HAPPENED TO me once, so I could relate.

That dull, anxious feeling, when all the carefully-prepared plans collapsed due to an unanticipated emergency. On the one hand, a very important work task demanding my full attention. On the other hand—actually, *in* the other hand—our pre-school kid.

Early on a Tuesday morning in the fall of 1975. Sherri, then about six months pregnant with our daughter, headed off to work at a women's health clinic, while I finished dressing our three-year-old son and prepared to drop him off at the babysitter's house. I would continue on to Hilbert College, where I taught a weekly course in Judaism. Sherri and I shared parenting tasks, with a complicated schedule, but one that flowed smoothly.

Zack's nursery school was closed that morning. No problem. He adored our sitter and her two daughters, and looked forward to spending the day with them. The three-hour class I taught began at 9 a.m. Sherri left early for her downtown

office, and at 7:45 a.m. Zack and I would head out to the suburbs, where I'd drop him at Roxanne's house and continue
for another 45 minutes along the expressway to the college in
Hamburg, N.Y.

A routine operation, well-orchestrated, with all bases
covered.

Until the phone rang. Shortly after Sherri left, an apologetic
and very sick Roxanne called, suggesting that whatever came
over her during the night was not something she'd want to
share with our child.

I agreed.

Now it was time to panic. We had no back-up sitters for
that time of day, and my students would be at their desks at 9,
most of them reasonably prepared to take the mid-term exam.
It would be unfair to postpone the test.

"Zack," I announced, "you're coming to school with Daddy."

I grabbed a supply of toys and books and crayons and
loaded them and Zack into the car. An hour later I handed
out the mid-term exams to my students with a three-year-old
playing caveman under my desk. I clearly recall the earnest
silence of the room being broken by a loud, "I got to pee"
coming from somewhere near my left foot.

That was my most memorable moment from the years of
juggling parenting and career though, of course, there were
others. Complications arise more and more these days, a result
of the new realities in family structures.

For Joan O'Gorman, it was much, much more complex and
challenging.

Joan was the minister of what used to be a small church
in the sleepy little village of East Arlington, Vermont, about
twenty minutes south of our town. After Joan assumed the
pulpit, the place grew tremendously, with people coming from
near and far to avail themselves of Joan's skills, creativity, and
warmth.

A while back, Joan told this story. It's a story that, in an
elegantly simple way teaches volumes about the mourning

process, the expression of grief and the way we grown-ups can, and occasionally should, perceive ourselves.

It was a situation very similar to the one I encountered on that mid-autumn day way back in Buffalo: important work, no babysitter available and, unexpectedly, a kid in tow. Only for Joan, it was worse. Much worse.

Her husband and older children were out of town, and her five-year-old had returned from his half-day of kindergarten. Joan decided to work at home, since it seemed to be a rather quiet day. Until the phone rang.

It was the funeral director, informing Joan that one of her oldest congregants had passed away. Joan scheduled the time for the memorial service and took care of a few other details, and then phoned the survivor.

There was only one survivor: the woman's son, a widower himself. He and his mother had lived together for years, until she entered the nursing home where she died in her mid-90s. Joan knew the man well, knew he'd be alone at his home where he spent most of the time. He had some acquaintances but few, if any, friends, and no close relatives. Joan realized that she should visit him. Soon. Now, in fact. It was the right thing to do.

But what about her little boy? No alternative. She would need to take him with her.

During the short drive, Joan gently tried to explain to her son how important it was that he behave especially, especially well. How important it was that he sit quietly, politely, and that if he acted like a big boy, they would stop at the Dairy Queen on the way home.

The son of the deceased was an elderly man, somewhere in his seventies. A grizzled native Vermonter, with strong hands and dark, leathery skin, he was what we affectionately call "a real woodchuck." He'd spent much of his life plowing snow, logging trees, doing carpentry and other outdoor work. He was a fisherman and a deer hunter. Intensely private, not given to small talk or any kind of talk at all.

They sat in the kitchen around the small table: Joan, her five-year-old, and the old man. Joan said all the appropriate things.

"I'm so sorry to hear about your mother, Don."

"Well," he responded, "she lived a pretty good life, at least 'til near the end."

Joan added, "I saw her last Monday at the nursing home. She had become very weak, but even then, still so gracious."

"Ayuh," he said. "Mother was always fond of you."

The conversation continued in that mode for a while. The five-year-old, trying so hard, looked from one adult face to the other, then gazed about the room at the ancient refrigerator and woodstove, the worn rocker with newspapers that lay across the ottoman. He was too small for the chair. His little legs swung back and forth, back and forth, until Joan gently rested her hand on his knee.

The old man rose slowly and walked stiffly to the cupboard. Without saying a word, he brought down a bag of Oreo cookies, placed them on the table, and gestured, with an open palm, that the boy might want some. Joan gave a nod of permission, and soon little hands and a little mouth were covered with chocolate crumbs.

The conversation continued. Laconic. Proper.

"Is there anything I can do for you, Don?" the minister asked.

"Oh, no. I'll be fine. Ya' know. This is life. Ya' got to expect these things."

Not much more to say. Joan was relieved. Her son had behaved well, she had done what was caring and proper, and now the visit seemed about to end.

The old man sat, watching, as Joan reached for a napkin and began to wipe her son's face and hands. The room was quiet.

And then for the first time, for the only time, the child spoke. He spoke like a five-year-old, unguarded, direct.

Looking straight up at the old man, he cocked his head to the side just a bit, wrinkled his nose, and said, "Mister, I'm sorry your mommy died."

The old man was silent. Lowered his head. And began to cry.

Somehow the simple language of a five-year-old eloquently evoked the pain in his heart. Yes, he was in his 70s, and his mother over 90.

But at that moment he was a little boy whose mommy had died.

CHAPTER 19

The Most Wonderful Day of My Entire Life

"MADAM, I HAVE never owned a Christmas tree that lost its needles."

Well, it was an honest reply to a customer's question. She was trying to decide between a Douglas fir and a balsam, and she asked her friendly salesman which would shed its needles first. I didn't bother to tell her I am a rabbi, and that I never owned a tree, period. Both of my fellow workers hid their smiles in their gloves, chuckling. Later, we let our customer in on the joke.

What was a rabbi doing selling Christmas trees on a Sunday afternoon in front of the bank in a small Vermont town? I'm a member of our Rotary Club, and this was one of our prime fund-raisers. Part of the profits are sent to the local food cupboard, and the remainder added to the club's college scholarship program.

Rotary is where I met Ferd Thoma. He was a senior member, a proud "old timer" who, at the time I joined, had ended his twenty-five-year perfect attendance streak and came to our weekly dinner meetings infrequently because of deteriorating health. A dark, short man with a bad limp requiring the assistance of a cane, Ferd's stocky physique was most likely an elderly version of muscular. He always wore an old maroon polyester sports coat, a wide, flowery tie, and a graying shirt. And he spoke with an elegant Hungarian accent.

And oh, did Ferd speak! He was a talker who loved sharing adventures from his past, his youth in World War II Budapest when he helped the legendary Raoul Wallenberg rescue tens of thousands of Jews. Ferd's accent was thick and melodious, as he told his tales and referred to documents—or, as he pronounced the word, "doc-ooo-ments"—attesting to this or that exploit.

Ferd lived up the mountain in an apartment over the ski store he and his late wife ran for decades. Now closed, Ferd's shop was a place, they say, where the kids from our town would buy their skis and boots and poles, and no matter how much money—or how little—the children had, each would emerge from Ferd's fully equipped. That's the way Ferd did business.

But by the time I got to know him, Ferd was ill, isolated, and pretty lonely up on the mountain. So it was a special treat for him to attend an occasional Rotary meeting. People there listened to his stories.

Winter in Vermont isn't so much harsh as it is long. We love the snow, the bracing cold, and the occasional storms that permit us to cancel plans and sit by the fire. The bigger storms come with bragging rights to our friends in more temperate zones, the folks who tease us about our weather as they dodge hurricanes, tornadoes, forest fires, floods and earthquakes.

But by late March and into April we've had enough, and outdoor activities in moderate temperatures become more appealing. Activities like the Loyalty Day Parade.

We hold the Loyalty Day Parade on the Sunday nearest May 1st, a time when we can pull out the light windbreakers and shake off the final frost. It's not a huge event—small communities don't engage in extravaganzas—but more of a slapped-together procession around town, with kids and adults marching up and down the few streets in our commercial district behind the volunteer fire company's trucks and perhaps an antique car's horn offering an aaah-ooooh-gah now and then.

The Rotary Club usually provides a "float." Occasionally it's a flat bed truck occupied by a few of our members, but most years it's just somebody's convertible, with the top down and some paper flowers stuck onto the front of the hood.

One year, Ferd rode in the convertible.

A few days before the parade, a member of the club who had a special fondness for Ferd called to ask him if he'd like to ride in the Rotary float. Of course, he was delighted. Tara drove up the mountain and brought Ferd down to the high school parking lot, just in time for the beginning of the forty-minute parade. The old man sat in the back of the Rotary car, alone, in his maroon polyester jacket and wide pastel tie, beaming. With a brief siren and a few throaty toots from the fire engine, the procession lurched forward, passed down Main Street, through "Malfunction Junction," and up to the Chittenden Bank, where it ended.

As the car slowly rolled along, a grinning Ferd turned from side to side, waving gently to the adults and the children and the babies in strollers lined along the sidewalks. And almost as soon as the parade began, it was over. The groups disbanded, decorations were stuffed in trash containers, and participants and spectators stood in small clumps, chatting with one another, making their plans for the rest of the balmy afternoon. Ferd was helped from the convertible and stood, leaning on his cane, speaking with old friends who were happy to see him in town.

On the way home, as Tara drove Ferd back up the mountain to his apartment above the shuttered ski shop, Ferd was contemplative, cheerful, and somewhat overwhelmed. Still hampered by an immigrant's difficulty with English, his unique garrulousness was replaced that afternoon by unusual moments of silence and a special look of pleasure, a constant smile as he gazed out the car window at the valley opening up to view through the breaks in the trees. He seemed to be trying to put his thoughts together. And finally, he succeeded.

"This day," he said, carefully choosing his words, "this day was the most *waanderful* day of my entire life." He paused. Then continued. "To think. To think. The entire town gave a parade. Just for me."

Until the day he died, two years later, Ferd continued to reminisce about that parade, about the day when the entire town gave a parade, just for him.

Nobody ever told him any different.

CHAPTER 20

The Miraculous Mezuzah

DIXIE.

That's what it is. The song, *Dixie*, as in "*I wish I was in the land of cotton. Old times they are not forgotten. Look away. Look away. Look away. Dixie land.*"

OK. I identified the song. But where is it coming from in this darkness? The notes sound electronic, a tinny, high-pitched tone.

I lift my head from the pillow and catch sight of the red numbers of an electric clock. 3:51. It must be 3:51 in the morning then. And where am I? Oh, right. In bed. In a hotel room.

In Moscow.

But *Dixie*? Why *Dixie*? Unless ... of course. One of the watches buried in my suitcase had gone off, serenading me in the midst of a deep sleep during which the power of exhaustion had overwhelmed the power of anxiety. The watches were gifts for the Mendeleev boys. Electronic watches with all kinds of gizmos, including, on one of them, a musical alarm. That's what aroused me at 3:51 a.m. in a Moscow hotel in April, 1983.

My rabbinical school classmate Leigh Lerner was asleep in another room down the corridor. Many hours earlier he had departed from his home in St. Paul, Minnesota, and I from Philadelphia. We met in Frankfurt, then flew into Moscow for a weeklong Passover visit with refuseniks, Jews who had declared their intention to leave Mother Russia but had been denied permission to depart.

Those were watershed years for the Jews of Russia. For decades, under anti-religious Communism, synagogues, Jewish schools, newspapers, social and cultural organizations had been methodically closed and practicing Jews intimidated, a calculated attempt to destroy the soul of Judaism in that country.

But in 1965, Elie Wiesel, reporting for an Israeli newspaper, traveled to the Soviet Union to discover, to his astonishment, that these religiously unschooled, isolated Jews had not lost their connection to the Jewish people. Surprisingly, and despite it all, they yearned somehow to recapture their magnificent heritage. He produced a slim volume called *The Jews of Silence.*

It was not, however, the Jews he'd visited whom he called silent, but Jews in the free world who were ignoring the plight of our trapped sisters and brothers. We were the Jews of silence. Soon the Soviet Jewry Movement began, organizing a human lifeline between free and oppressed Jewish communities.

That's how Leigh and I came to Moscow. As ambassadors. Teachers. Pack mules.

This last function was the most important as well as the most dangerous. The Soviet government, at that time under Yuri Andropov, did not look favorably upon citizens who openly declared that religious freedom was more important than the great privilege of living under Communism. Refuseniks were continually harassed, imprisoned, fired from their jobs, kicked out of schools and sometimes physically assaulted. With rare exceptions, they were not allowed to leave the country.

Leigh and I arrived in Moscow with heavy suitcases and departed Leningrad nearly empty. Along our way we distributed books and toys, clothing and religious items to the people we visited. My inspection at Moscow's airport was rigorous.

"Why all the books?"

"I read a lot."

"And the baby's bib with *Shalom* written across it?"

"For a friend in Helsinki, my next stop."

The agent instructed me to empty both of my suitcases while alerting his boss.

"What are these?" the supervisor asked, pointing to a handful of *mezuzot* (plural of *mezuzah*,) small, sacred objects containing verses from the Torah and placed on the doorposts of Jewish homes.

"Good luck charms," I replied, attempting to use humor as a way of distracting him. "I'm afraid of flying. And they worked! The plane didn't crash!" He was not amused.

"Any other books?" he asked, surveying my two-foot pile.

"No," I replied, hoping he wouldn't find the three small Russian-Hebrew *Haggadahs*, Passover prayer books I had placed in my jacket pocket half a world earlier. If the *Haggadahs* were discovered I knew I'd be in for some trouble. After all, the Russians were none too keen on Jewish readings celebrating human freedom. But with a final suspicious glare the supervisor walked away; the inspector allowed me to repack and waved me through where I caught up with a slightly less harassed Leigh.

The next day, while visiting with a Moscow refusenik family, I was shown four 8-by-10 glossy photographs of book pages that served as their ersatz Passover guide. I gave them one of my precious contraband *Haggadahs*.

During that first encounter with refuseniks, and all through the week, I kept thinking about one of my favorite childhood books, Nathan Ausubel's *A Treasury of Jewish Folklore*. It was a compendium of true stories and legends, with separate sections on people who were wise, people who were holy, or witty, or droll. There were chapters on righteous men and women, on martyrs, on the charitable and the mystics.

But my favorite, the one to which I returned again and again, was the section entitled *Fighters and Strong Men*. Included among the "men" was the apocryphal story of how Judith slew the Greek general Holofernes, as well as accounts of Judah Maccabee, the Warsaw Ghetto resistance, and Hymie Epstein, a medical aide who sacrificed his life rescuing his fellow soldiers in a World War II Pacific battle.

In Moscow I thought: As a kid I read about Jewish heroes. Now I am meeting them, in person. Real heroes. The *Fighters and Strong Men*. I am meeting them, face to face.

And who were they, these people of courage who defied the foreboding power of the Soviet Union, who quietly, and sometimes not so quietly, demonstrated contempt for the Communist totalitarian system? They were mathematicians and pediatricians, engineers and scientists, teachers and architects. Heroes. Strong men and women. Remarkably, surprisingly ordinary people risking, and often losing, everything in pursuit of freedom and dignity.

Leigh and I spent time with the mathematician/pediatrician couple whose twin sons were fast approaching military age. We sat with the engineer who told us of his gruesome year in a prison, punishment for attending a lecture on Jewish philosophy. And we exchanged jokes and sang songs in a living room full of people whose simple social gathering their country begrudged them.

But the most eminent and the most interesting of the refuseniks we met was the scientist. It took forever to reach his home by subway, then taxi. He lived with his wife and two teenage children in a distant Moscow suburb. By Russian standards theirs was a comfortable, modern apartment, built for prominent people like himself. Only he was no longer very prominent. He was an outcast.

For years the scientist headed a prestigious research institute. He was a brilliant man, well known in international scientific circles. But there came a point in his life when he decided that the Soviet Union was not the place in which he wished to live, and that as Jews, he and his wife and especially his children would be far better off in a place more hospitable to their people.

As soon as he announced his intentions to leave, he was fired from his position and continually harassed by the KGB. His applications to depart were invariably denied, placing him and his family in refusenik limbo. Visitors like us became his lifeline, with international attention serving as his safety net against more punitive actions by the authorities.

We learned all this during a leisurely afternoon meal in the living room/dining room that also served as the master bedroom. Russian luxury.

In his excellent English, the scientist related precisely the details of his odyssey from internationally respected scholar to pariah, the penalty for claiming his fundamental right to religious freedom. He was not self-pitying. Rather, he approached his situation analytically, speaking of cause and effect, actions and reactions, choices and the ramifications of those choices.

Still, there was a sadness, a constant, obvious fear, a sense of loneliness and loss, painful byproducts of following one's conscience in the Soviet Union.

A few weeks prior to our arrival the authorities paid one of their frequent, unannounced visits to the scientist's home. They were annoyed with him. He was becoming a *cause celebre*, his name even appearing in an impassioned column by Anthony Lewis of *The New York Times*. It's not good public relations, they told him, for westerners to read how Russia torments intellectuals unwilling to bear with the system. Keep your mouth shut, they warned him, or we'll take away your library privileges. Stop meeting with Jews and others from abroad.

A serious threat. Banned from the institute he once headed, the man subsequently channeled his genius into historical research as a means of remaining sharp in his field despite the ostracism. Library privileges were essential. Their loss would be devastating.

But capitulation to the KGB was out of the question. He took the risk, and warmly welcomed us as guests in his apartment.

We spent hours at that dining table, eating and drinking and exchanging pleasantries. But primarily Leigh and I simply listened to the scientist and his wife relate their story. The telling, for them, was part self-defense and also, unquestionably, part therapy.

We were not particularly relaxed. A third presence hovered about continually: the uninvited guest, the interloper, the eavesdropper. Refuseniks took it for granted that their homes were bugged. Some were perpetually fearful. Others, like the scientist, openly and boldly contemptuous.

In the midst of our visit there was a knock on the door.

We had been prepared for this. We knew that occasionally the KGB or the police interrupted gatherings such as ours, sometimes kicking the visitors out of the country and imprisoning the hosts on trumped-up charges. More often, though, it was just a way to unnerve people, to remind them that they were being monitored.

When we heard the knock our conversation ended abruptly. We looked at one other with shifting eyes and resigned expressions. No other guests had been expected, and any informal, friendly visits by neighbors had long been terminated, another of the byproducts of the paranoia surrounding this refusenik family.

Our hostess began to rise from her seat but her husband gently placed his hand on her arm. He would see who was knocking. As he walked to the front of the room and around the corner to the entrance way, I recalled what had happened three days earlier, when we first encountered the scientist on a Sabbath afternoon outside the large Moscow synagogue. I was speaking with some refuseniks when suddenly we heard shouting. Behind me the scientist was lambasting a man who quickly began to slink away. Later, the scientist modestly explained that the person he had denounced was an informer, and that an individual has two choices: either permit such traitors to do their "work" or expose them and drive them away, even if at personal risk.

We waited anxiously. Soon we heard a brief, muffled conversation, then the sound of the door closing.

The scientist returned to the room, a yellow paper in his hand and a huge smile across his face. He snapped to attention, uncrinkled the telegram, and began to read, "Warmest Passover wishes from your friends in Philadelphia." It was signed by two members of my synagogue who had traveled to Russia the previous year.

The remainder of the afternoon passed quickly, pleasantly. Leigh and I had another invitation for the evening and a long distance to travel back to the center of the city. Before we departed, though, we all participated in a quasi-ritual, an exchange of small gifts as a means of solidifying a relationship between people who care for one another's future but quite possibly would never meet again.

The scientist and his wife presented each of us with a set of beautiful Russian wooden folk art dolls. And we, in turn, asked if they would like us to affix a *mezuzah* to their entranceway doorframe. From my pocket I took one of the *mezuzot* I had finessed past the airport guard and placed it on the table between us. Our hosts were delighted. More than delighted. They asked what would be needed, and I explained only a hammer and some small nails.

It's interesting, over the course of years, what one remembers following an important encounter. Looking back to that afternoon, I can still feel the courage in the room, the powerful intellect, the anxiety, as well as the deep gratitude shown us. But what I see most clearly is the surprisingly boyish excitement in the scientist's manner as he literally jumped up from the table and raced into the pantry to fetch the tools. His whole demeanor changed; he seemed beside himself. He was joyful.

Given the scientist's background and the nature of Jewish life under Communism, it is quite possible that our affixing the *mezuzah* constituted the very first Jewish religious ceremony ever to take place in that home.

A *mezuzah* is ordinarily placed on the outside, upper right side of an entrance door. To avoid more harassment and vandalism, we creatively placed it inside the door. Leigh and I recited the traditional blessings, ending with the words, "May God watch over you when you go out and when you come in, now and always. Amen."

The scientist hammered the little nails, a bit clumsily. He was nervous, caught up in the moment. But he accomplished the task, and then just stood there, silent, looking at the addition to his apartment and nodding his head slowly, approvingly. Soon after, Leigh and I headed back into the center of Moscow, then to Leningrad, and finally, home to our families in America.

I corresponded with the scientist for a while. It almost made no sense to mail the letters since most were intercepted and destroyed. But through the lifeline of visitors we did manage to remain in touch. At one point I tried, unsuccessfully, to send him a badly needed word processor.

By the middle of the 1980s, international pressure had forced the Russians to open their gates slightly, and Jews were dribbling out. "Yes," the Kremlin reluctantly announced, "we will respect the desire of some to leave our country." At the same time, though, they published a list of eight people—eight particularly "valuable" people—whom they said they would absolutely never allow to leave. The scientist was on the list.

The subtleties and complexities of international relations have always confused me. I have never quite understood just how events in that arena develop. At the same time, there is very little of the mystic in me. I'm a rationalist, not very superstitious, routinely skeptical of unusual turns of events, preferring to credit coincidence rather than something otherworldly.

That's why it felt very strange, late in the 1980s, to find myself sitting in a Philadelphia hotel eating breakfast with a local friend active in the cause of Soviet Jewry and our two guests. The scientist and his wife.

It was a joyful reunion, a celebration of their release into a new, productive life of freedom. We spoke of the years of our connectedness, and they filled in the details of their final years in Russia as well as their liberation. There was a sense of unreality that morning. After all that had happened, here we were, face to face over waffles and coffee in a Philadelphia restaurant.

But what remains with me most clearly is something the scientist told me just as we were about to say goodbye. What he related goes against my logical nature, and probably goes against his scientific nature. I have meditated on what he told me that day ever since hearing it.

Almost embarrassed, with a slightly quizzical grin on his face, the modern-day fighter and strong man shared one last detail of his story:

From the moment, years earlier, when we affixed the *mezuzah*, until the day he and his family left Russia, the KGB never returned to their home.

CHAPTER **21**

The Puppy in the Pew

SHE COULD DEFINITELY become an auctioneer, I thought. Maybe a cheerleader, or even an opera singer, blessed as she was with an exceptionally powerful set of lungs.

But at the time I encountered her, in an airport boarding area, Lydia was 10 months old. And she was screaming. Not the typical crabby-baby-gimme-a-bottle squeal, but a full-throated, high-pitched and remarkably sustained shriek, of which few infants are fully capable. It wasn't a sign of discomfort. The little cutie was smiling. She just enjoyed letting loose.

As a frequent flyer, I had "status," allowing me to board the Philadelphia-London flight early and settle into my prized exit row aisle seat. I shut down my phone, then watched the line of incoming passengers, guarding my head each time a suddenly pivoting, oblivious person wearing a backpack neared me. And in my mind, the thought, "Oh please! Don't let this family sit near me! Seven hours and fifteen minutes with Lydia?"

The four of them—mom, dad, well-behaved little boy, and Lydia—ended up just two rows behind me. I slouched in my seat listening to the continuing intermittent screams, and prepared for a really uncomfortable journey.

Then I felt a tap on my shoulder. Turning my head, I found myself face-to-face with Lydia's father. In his hand, an open box, filled with an array of colorful earplugs. I began to laugh, and he assured me that "there's an 85 percent chance that she'll sleep the whole way." I chose a pair of the plugs, thanked him for his sensitivity, and watched as he continued making his rounds.

Lydia, as he predicted, fell asleep before takeoff and was still dozing as her dad carried her off the plane at Heathrow.

Just to be safe, though, I bought a headset in case Lydia awakened. The movie turned out to be decent, and it was followed by a succession of short subjects: an episode of a sitcom, something about endangered tigers, plus a lecture by psychologist Daniel Goleman. I was about to shut down the video and turn my attention to the latest John Grisham novel, but surprisingly, Goleman grabbed my full attention, driving me ultimately to rustle quickly inside my airplane bag in search of pen and paper.

Goleman's presentation was simple. It was eloquent. It was meaningful. Concluding his remarks, he observed, "We all have the power … we all have the power ... to make each other feel better or worse."

Hearing those few words, that succinct observation, made the long night's flight especially worthwhile. "We all have the power to make each other feel better or worse."

It was the end of February, and Sherri and I had decided to take separate vacations. Sherri spends her days and weeks with clients in psychotherapy sessions. What she wanted more than anything else was a very empty, very quiet beach. I, on the other hand, work alone in my home office when not performing stand-up comedy. A healthy break for me requires things to do, places to visit, people to meet.

So Sherri and our daughter flew to Anguilla in the Caribbean for a few days. I flew alone to London, and, as planned, ten minutes after my arrival at Heathrow, our son, an antsy type like his father, emerged from a different airplane, meeting me just beyond customs.

We had a great time sightseeing, attending shows and museums, and eating together, then going off on our own at other times, to pursue our varied interests.

For me: a semi-busman's holiday.

On Sunday morning, I went to the famous St. Martin-in-the-Fields Anglican Church. Lovers of fine music will recognize that name: it sometimes seems that half of all recorded classical music is produced by "Sir Neville Mariner and the St. Martin-in-the Fields Chorus and Orchestra" or some combination thereof.

I anticipated that the music would be splendid, and it was. The worship was richly ceremonial, further confirming my expectations.

Then came time for the sermon, what I figured would be a combination of formal erudition delivered in crisp, dulcet tones. We all watched as the vicar climbed the twelve steps up into the high pulpit. Once ensconced, he began, "Moses descended the moun-tain, carrying the Lawh of the Lawd. And when he reached the Children of Is-ra-ail, he said unto them, 'I have good news and bahd news. The good news is, there are only ten com-mahnd-ments. The bahd news is, Adultery is forbidden.'" Laughter echoed off the centuries-old walls.

I chatted with the vicar afterward. A lovely man, deeply committed to Jewish-Christian understanding and to the homeless shelter run by his congregation.

And his sermon reminded me: everyone's a comedian.

Shabbat provided yet another opportunity for meeting colleagues who combined lovely worship services with personal warmth and good humor.

Rabbi Mark Winer served the prestigious West London Synagogue at the time. Mark was a transplanted American, a towering fellow who stands about 6-6. While introducing the visiting speaker, a German rabbi who was nearly as tall, Mark remarked, "It's good to finally have as our guest a normal-size rabbi."

The West London Synagogue is located in a prestigious neighborhood. The outside, like many European synagogues, is nondescript, even hard to find. But the interior is ornate, embracing, impressive, lovely. Dark wood, splendid tapestries, high spaces, history oozing from all sections. And the music: the music on that ordinary Shabbat was, to me, extraordinary.

But my most significant memory was not the worship service, or the sermon, or the building, or the music.

It was the lady with the dog.

I walked in early, and took a seat near the rear so I could admire the elaborate architecture and décor. I read the service leaflet, and eavesdropped on a very British conversation behind me, with a young woman addressing the older man next to her as "Sir Jacob." People continued to filter in. A few engaged in quiet conversation, while others took their seats in silence.

I felt a presence approaching from behind my aisle seat, and, looking slightly over my shoulder, watched from the corner of my eye as a woman walked abreast of me, continued ahead, and turned left, stepping up onto the riser and moving into the pew directly in front.

Quite elderly, frail, thin, she wore a threadbare cloth coat, a scarf, and a small hat. And she was stooped over. Completely stooped over, her body condemned to nearly a 90-degree angle. Bad osteoporosis, it must have been. She was all alone.

At least that's what I thought, until I saw the plaid leash in her hand, and, following it downward, realized that she was accompanied by a small dog with curly gray hair and a speck of white on its little nose.

I'm not overly fond of small dogs. I like the larger guys, the ones you can take a hike with, wrestle with, the ones big enough to be able to pretend to protect you. Little yappy pooches that bark their shrill, incessant complaints are just not my type.

But this diminutive pup didn't fit my admittedly biased stereotype. He was kind of cute, and, more important, docile. Just sat there, on the floor or on the seat next to his mistress, moving around occasionally, but nary a whimper, not even a proper British "woof."

The old woman couldn't seem to get comfortable, or decide what to do. In the minutes preceding the beginning of the service, she slowly, almost painfully, made her way out of the sanctuary with the dog, then returned, then walked out and back in again. Always to the same seats, in front of me.

And I began to think: this is really strange! I wonder if she's a street person, someone who simply followed the open door into the synagogue, or maybe she's a long-time member, an institution herself, within a venerable institution.

I also thought, how appropriate that this woman should have a little dog to accompany her, to occupy her, to love her. After all, her body is condemned to being so bent. With effort she can look straight ahead; otherwise, her face is downcast. Always looking at the ground. Always looking at the floor. Always looking at … the loving, liquid little eyes of her adoring puppy.

But still: a dog on Shabbat at the West London Synagogue? Was this right?

Just before the service began, I received my answer. A few people were still filing in as the rabbi, synagogue leaders, and the guest speaker began to emerge from a door behind the high pulpit. Standing down below, in the front of the sanctuary, a dapper looking man, one who seemed very much at home in this place, surveyed the congregation. I saw his eyes stop when he noticed the old lady and her dog. He continued to look at her, and began to walk purposefully in our direction. This will be revealing, I thought. This will certainly be interesting.

I sat quietly, trying to look as if I were minding my own business, pretending to simply await the beginning of the service while, in reality, intensely interested in the little drama about to take place five feet in front of me.

The man marched up the aisle, his face a mask of neutrality, betraying neither anger nor amusement. As he drew closer, he looked continually toward the shabbily dressed old woman and her dog, now nestled beside her on the pew. Finally reaching her, he stopped, paused for a moment, took in the entire scene, and then addressed her with a slight smile: "Why," he began, "your lipstick is a particularly lovely shade this evening, matching your coat in a most fetching way. You do look quite enchanting!"

He bid her "Good Shabbos," a good Sabbath, then did an about face, returned to his seat, and the service began.

Choices. For evil or for good. To hurt or to heal, to curse or to bless. These choices are very much in our hands, every day, every single moment of our lives.

USAirways Flight 98, hurtling toward London over the dark waters of the North Atlantic. A still cabin, silent except for the engine noises. And from the screen hanging from the ceiling, Daniel Goleman's words of enlightenment, clarity, inspiration. Words of ultimate truth.

"We all have the power," he reminds us, "to make each other feel better or worse."

CHAPTER 22

A Wounded Father

THE PHOTO WAS definitely a surprise, something I'd never even imagined.

It was an old, tattered, black and white picture, vaguely out of focus, showing a laughing man, perhaps about 30, mugging for the photographer, and a woman looking at him, a large, admiring grin across her face. She wears a long plaid dress in the style of the 1950s, but he's attired in dark shoes, black socks, a sweater and a porkpie hat. And no pants. Instead, he seems to be wrapped in a small sheet that looks like a disheveled skirt. They were having a great time.

It's a remarkable photo, shining light on a time when my wife's parents could smile, obviously enjoying the moment, perhaps even enjoying life in general.

A surprise, because that's not how I experienced them. To me, Sherri's father was laconic, guarded, tense, introverted. And most of all, wounded.

John grew up in a modest household in which he and his two sisters and brother were raised by their warm and loving

Polish immigrant parents. John married Sherri's mother, Dorothy, and life proceeded normally until their world began to collapse when Sherri was in second grade and her sister in kindergarten. That year saw the beginning of Dorothy's severe mental illness.

I entered their family circle just as Sherri was graduating from high school, making my nervous appearances while fetching Sherri for dates, and spending what seemed to be interminably long minutes with John as I awaited her. Over the next five years the discomfort never lessened, though both John and I learned to focus our infrequent conversations on the family's beloved, attention-diverting toy fox terrier, who loathed me.

The week after Sherri and I were married, John took me as a guest to his Rotary Club barbecue. My new gold wedding ring was so shiny it nearly blinded people in the afternoon sunlight. It was at a point when Sherri's mother was particularly ill, and I wondered if showing off his daughter's new husband to his friends was a bright spot in an especially desolate time.

John was suffering. The hope and promise, the reciprocal joy depicted in that old photo, had long disappeared, replaced by the heartbreak and loss that happens when one lover leaves the other, against both of their wills, to travel to a land of permanent paranoia and depression.

Over those years, Sherri transitioned from being a dutiful child, responsible well beyond her years, to a helpful adolescent daughter, and finally, soon after we were married, to her mother's sole caregiver. Dorothy lived in nursing homes near us for 25 years, until she died.

I've often wondered about this wounded man whom I knew so superficially. I wondered what he was like before his life destructed and his dreams were ravaged.

Apparently he cared for Sherri, appreciated her, loved her, though he simply couldn't express it in traditional terms. But in one memorable instance, he did.

John worked hard throughout his life. During the time I knew him he was a plant engineer for a paper company and, later, for a book printing factory. Expenses associated with Dorothy's illness, and the reality of living a solitary life within their joyless marriage, left John with no luxuries and few pleasures. Except for a used Thunderbird. It was John's prized distraction: white exterior, aqua upholstery, a powerful engine, and a steering wheel that moved to the side as the driver entered and exited. Driving the Thunderbird transformed him from the powerless husband of a mentally ill woman to a man who was somebody.

With so little happiness in his life, the car was his most cherished possession. Still, he let Sherri drive it while she was home on a college break.

Sherri understood how much the car meant to her father. When she backed the Thunderbird out of a narrow parking space, ultimately rubbing along a too-nearby light pole and placing both a long scratch and huge dent on the car's right side, she panicked, fearing she had ruined her father's most important pleasure in his otherwise bleak life.

She came into their apartment weeping, finding her father sitting alone in their small living room, TV quietly playing in the background. During her drive home, Sherri rehearsed how she'd break the awful news to him, but when the moment came, the words were nearly incomprehensible, spoken as they were between her enormous sobs.

Sherri finally poured out the details, then continued to cry. All these years later, she's never forgotten his reaction, the response from this laconic man, this guarded, intense, unexpressive man. This wounded man.

"Are you OK?" he asked. And she nodded, expecting anger. And hurt. And disappointment. Instead, he simply smiled in relief, raised his eyebrow ever so slightly, and said, quietly, "It's just a goddam car."

Forty-five years later, "It's just a goddam car" still echoes. There are many ways to say, "I love you."

CHAPTER 23

About Men

HE LIVES ABOUT a mile up our road, which, in our corner of Vermont, qualifies him as one of our closest neighbors.

Jim, one could say, has it all. Probably in his mid-fifties, he's "ruggedly handsome," according to a magazine article about his wife, Nancy, an attractive blonde, who used to model for clothing catalogs, but whose main profession is oil painting. Her work is magnificent. About twenty years ago, she won a prestigious competition that catapulted her to national fame. Jim managed her career for a while, and then returned to his own career as a sports medicine orthopedist at a hospital and a ski resort.

They travel widely, live in an expansive old farmhouse, raise sheep and two exotic Highland cows, and, from my vantage point, seem to enjoy a pretty idyllic life.

Except for one thing: a few years ago, Jim developed prostate cancer.

Jim's a physician, but is also very much what one terms "a man's man." He loves fishing and hunting and other outdoor activities. Works the woods and fields around his house. He usually sports a deep tan and calloused hands.

Soon after Jim was diagnosed with prostate cancer, soon after he underwent surgery, he did something remarkable: he established a support program for men with his disease. And he didn't do it in a quiet, mousy, squeamish way. He went public, big time. One morning I opened *The Rutland Herald*, our local daily, and found a huge, half-page photo of seven smiling men, including Jim and his older brother, inviting others to join their group for men battling prostate cancer.

A few months later, Jim asked me to do some stand-up comedy at one of their monthly gatherings. Their agendas are, understandably, serious. Jim felt that healthy laughter would provide a nice break in their routine.

Funny thing is, when I arrived at the meeting place and was introduced to the men, most asked me, with conspiratorial-ly-raised eyebrows, "Are you a member of the fraternity?" In other words, do you have prostate cancer too?

"No," I answered, and somewhere inside me, for just a flash of a second, I felt a strange, maybe bizarre, yet also understandable twinge: They "belong." I don't.

Nor, of course, would I wish to be eligible to join that club. The price of admission is far too high.

But sitting there, that night, at such a rare kind of event, reminded me of the loneliness that is part of being a man in our society.

Not so for most women. Sharon, the woman who used to cut my hair, received her diagnosis of breast cancer a few years ago. Everybody copes with horrific news in different ways. Sharon addressed her fear and anger, of course, but she also gained admission to a new sorority whose sole function is to befriend and nurture women in their crises. She joined the breast cancer support group which my wife, Sherri, a psychotherapist, facilitates. When radiation took her hair, Sharon wore a hat for a couple of days and then removed it, proclaiming her bald head as a badge of honor and a symbol of her determination to survive.

On the day of the Race for the Cure, a major cancer fundraising event in our town, Sharon proudly wore her pink T-shirt, as did all of the women fighting the disease, while Sherri and I wore the white and blue shirts of volunteers.

Sharon reveled in her role as part of the group. The price was high, too high, but how marvelous, how absolutely marvelous, that all of these opportunities were available for her: a chance to avoid the isolation of illness, to find and receive comfort, and most important, to keep her spirits high, a critical asset in confronting any disease.

Yes, women know how to nurture each other.

And for men? For a rural location, our community was fortunate to have the group Jim started. In more populous places, care is offered through outreach by hospitals and The American Cancer Society's *Man To Man* program. Helpful, certainly. Nourishing, I'm sure, for some.

But basically, only a tiny step.

Can one imagine thousands of people marching in the fight against prostate cancer, with men who have survived wearing special T-shirts? Can one imagine an impotence support group, or an organization to help men who are emotionally closed-off? How about group therapy sessions for workaholics, or a "sons of abusive fathers" support series?

Men don't do it. We haven't yet learned from women how to take care of ourselves emotionally.

Of course, there are fads that pop up for a few heady years, like the old Promise Keepers, the organization founded by a football coach that brought hundreds of thousands of men into stadiums to repent and weep and hug and then return home where they were supposed to promise to spend more time with their subservient wives.

David Crumm, my friend and editor at ReadTheSpirit, spent decades covering religious life in America, including the meteoric rise of Promise Keepers. After following the group for a while, he reported that The Promise Keepers are "men who couldn't express their faith unless they were standing in a stadium with a coach telling them it's OK."

Of late there have been some New Age attempts at providing serious emotional bonding for men. Some are kind of funny: beating on drums was the rage a few years ago. And in our area, so I hear, there's a group of men who retreat to sweat lodges, where they sit around, naked and perspiring, sharing deep thoughts.

Not my cup of herbal tea.

There's so much men can learn from the women who surround us, and from the women's movement. Sure, women are from Venus and men are from Mars. We have different natures, different approaches to life, different coping skills. But men ought to pay more attention to what women are doing. Support groups; intense, nurturing, deep friendships; self-revelation in settings that feel safe, unthreatening, noncompetitive.

It's time men began offering more than lip service to the ideal of elevating family over career, of attending to our emotional well-being with the intensity that we channel toward achieving our vocational goals.

This is a slow, evolutionary process. Bit by bit, we take cautious steps in the right direction, whether through corporations mandating paternity leave for employees or on a more personal level, a dozen worried men, all dealing with prostate cancer, sitting in a conference room in a Vermont hospital, revealing their fear, sharing their hope.

That prostate cancer support group, of course, is an exception in what is still a "man's world."

This was poignantly symbolized for me by a scene I witnessed recently at O'Hare Airport, in a crowded United Airlines Club.

It was a typical late weekday afternoon crowd: mostly men, some talking on their cell phones, others pounding laptops or just sitting, looking exhausted, ties askew, checking the monitors for updates on their rain-delayed flights.

When a newly-arrived passenger grabbed a seat opposite me, I noticed a slight pause, and then he smiled and shook hands with the man sitting to his right. If I had to guess, I'd say that they had just attended a convention of their industry, but hadn't encountered each other until this moment.

I couldn't help overhearing the conversation. They began with the usual exchanges, generalities about business, about travel. And then, almost out of nowhere, one said to the other, in a more subdued voice, "You had a daughter who died, didn't you?"

"Yes," the second man replied. "She was twenty-two. A car accident, her last year in college." The banter around me, the conversations others were having, ceased. The two men didn't seem to notice.

The speaker continued. "It happened a year ago December. And you? You lost a child too, didn't you?"

"Yes. Also a daughter. She was a little younger than yours, just 19. Leukemia."

People dragging roll-on suitcases angled their way between furniture, searching for empty seats as the televisions reported news in the background. Those seated nearby, pretending to mind their own business, listened.

"It was hardest for my wife, you know. She's home all the time. At least I get to travel around."

"Yeah, it's tough. Really rough. I guess we'll get over it some day. Hope so."

And then, as quickly as the subject was raised, it was dropped, replaced by safe banter about little-known ways to grab first class upgrades or exit rows.

And at that moment I thought: here are two men in an airport lounge, now behaving the way men are expected to behave, exchanging information about travel and the weather. But what I was really witnessing was two gravely wounded souls, sharing similar agony, supportively interacting with one another only as intimately as our society permits men to do.

And it isn't very much.

What a chance missed to ease, even slightly, the heartbreak they shared.

But that's how men are. We're making some progress, slowly, with a long road yet to travel. A couple of steps forward, a step back. Human evolution is like that. First we develop the New Age, sensitive male. That's a couple of steps forward. Then the New Age sensitive male jumps a tad too far, and becomes the object of ridicule. One step back. And so it goes.

The hope is that by taking a look at ourselves as men, as 21st century American men, we will eventually be able to learn, to prioritize, to grow, and ultimately, to address effectively those elements that so often lie neglected at our spiritual and emotional core.

It's a new direction, an enhancement of our lives that we, even we men, deserve.

CHAPTER 24

Gerda's Grandfather

THEY ARE FAMILY relics, sacred heirlooms, about which we know so very little, about which as more years flow by, we know even less. Yet we hold onto them, an inheritance which we guard: boxes containing photographs, entrusted by most families to whoever, for a few years, occupies the status of "older generation."

For Sherri and me, included in that inevitable though undesired elevation to the older generation was the receipt of a pair of boxes of old photographs that had been in my mother's keeping ever since her parents and parents-in-law had died. Resting on a high shelf in our cellar, the boxes contain a collection of well-worn black and white pictures, some framed, some loose, most of them of individuals and groups of people whom I cannot place, though a few of the faces look eerily familiar.

But one large portrait from that collection, now framed, commands the gallery that lines the stairway to our second floor: my great-grandfather, Meyer Solomon Alper, who died long before I was born. He was a good-looking man who fled what was, for Jews, dangerous Lithuania. In 1882 he arrived in America, where he went from rag peddler to nationally prominent businessman. His expression, as in most photographs of his era, is unsmiling.

My friend Gerda Klein has a similar photo of an ancestor she never knew, her paternal grandfather. It depicts a man with a long, untrimmed gray beard, a high *yarmulke*, clenched fists, a stern, almost angry look across on face. Incongruously, the woman sitting to his right bears a slight smile, and the young woman standing behind him rests her hand on the old man's shoulder, affectionately.

Gerda is an inspiring and deeply beloved lecturer and author. Many recall her uniquely moving acceptance speech after the HBO documentary about her life *One Survivor Remembers* won an Oscar. Her heartbreaking, amazing story is featured in the film *Testimony*, shown at The United States Holocaust Memorial Museum in Washington, D.C. She is an honored recipient of our nation's highest civilian award, the Presidential Medal of Freedom.

But for me, Gerda is, simply, the most valued teacher in my life. She and gentle, poetic Kurt, her late husband, were members of my congregation in Buffalo during the 1970s, and it was there that I first learned the details of her extraordinary life. Raised in upper-middle-class privilege in a city on the Polish-Czech border, Gerda's idyllic childhood ended catastrophically, when World War II began. Her entire family was murdered by the Nazis and their accomplices. Gerda herself survived forced labor, concentration camps, and a death march, a march that began on the very day I was born, a world away. Gerda's tragedy and, more important, the lessons she teaches about the sanctity of life's most mundane pleasures, continue to influence my life deeply.

One of those lessons centers on what Gerda yearned for during her teenage years as a prisoner, especially during her months on that brutal forced march through frozen Europe as her companions perished one by one: she longed to spend what she called "a boring evening at home," just playing with her cat, watching as her mother knitted, as her father read the newspaper, as her brother prepared his homework.

Gerda has written nine books, of which the first and best known is *All But My Life,* now in its 68th printing. A more recent work is an inspiring collection of stories from her life, stories both old and recent. It's called *A Boring Evening At Home.*

As soon as it was published, Gerda thoughtfully sent me a copy. Of course, I read it right away, and then phoned Gerda.

"Thank you for the book. And thank you for the subject of my next Yom Kippur sermon."

To which she instantly replied, "My grandfather?"

"Yes," I answered. "Your grandfather."

I had often wondered: Gerda has meant so much to me: a guide, an inspiration, a sweet and caring friend. Was she ever as fortunate as I? Was there someone in her life who served as her guide and her inspiration? When I read one of the final chapters in her book, I discovered that she indeed had been blessed with such a person. Her grandfather. A man she never met. That seemingly elderly man with the long, gray beard, the high *yarmulke*, the clenched fists, the deeply serious expression. "He was my lodestar," Gerda explained.

Who was this man whose memory, whose life, sustained and encouraged Gerda throughout the years of darkness?

Less than a year old when her paternal grandfather died, Gerda did not know Reb Weissmann. Yet, she explains, he had more influence on her thoughts, particularly about religion, than anyone else.

Gerda relates the complex and moving story of her father, his parents and siblings during World War I. She focuses on her grandfather, a very pious man, well-deserving of the honored title "Reb," which is bestowed on respected teachers. Living in Czortkow, a *Fiddler On the Roof* kind of town in Poland, he went to the synagogue each day, but he also felt a deep appreciation of nature, enjoying animals and flowers and trees, reciting his prayers as he walked in the forest.

Early in the war, Czortkow was occupied by the Russian enemy. One day, as Reb Weissmann walked through the woods, he came upon a baby bird that had fallen from its nest, the mother bird hovering over it helplessly. He feared that if he touched the baby, the mother would reject it, so he found a fork-like branch, lifted the small bird, and replaced it in the nest.

At that same moment, a pair of drunk Russian soldiers spied Reb Weissmann. In short order, they accused him of being a spy, charging this man, who had never seen a telephone in his life, with putting up wires in trees to aid the enemy. He was quickly tried, convicted, and exiled to Siberia for the rest of his life.

Following a wrenching, tearful goodbye, he departed, bearing only a small sack with a few clothes, along with his sacred prayer shawl and his tattered prayer book. His family thought they might never see or hear from him again.

The war finally ended. Gerda's parents were married and settled in Gerda's mother's home city of Bielsko, over 700 kilometers from Czortkow.

And then one day, a nearly miraculous telegram arrived, announcing that Reb Weissmann had returned. He had simply appeared in the doorway of his home, much older looking, very thin, with a long gray beard. He had barely survived his incarceration and his year-long walk home across Russia, often near starvation, eating only the vegetables and the occasional fruit he could scrounge. Never, even in the most desperate times, did he eat non-kosher food.

As soon as they learned the astounding news, Gerda's parents made arrangements to travel to Czortkow as quickly as they could, not only to see Gerda's grandfather, but to introduce Gerda's mother and their first-born, Artur, to the Weissmann family.

In preparation for the journey, Gerda's mother and grandmother prepared a basket of their most delicious recipes, including baked goods and their famous chicken. Gerda's mother was nervous, understandably. She worried about what could be a clash of cultures, she a product of a sophisticated, cosmopolitan, liberal Jewish community and her husband's family, Orthodox Jews and far less worldly. Nor could she speak Yiddish, the language of the Weissmanns and their Czortkow community

It was understandably a highly emotional reunion.

And here's the part of the story I love, and the reason I chose to include this story in a sermon I delivered on Yom Kippur, the most solemn day of the Jewish year. It tells of an electric confrontation and of a remarkable man, whose sensitivity we might all remember and emulate.

It was time to eat, time for Gerda's mother to present to her husband's family the special delicacies she had brought with her. In her mother-in-law's strictly kosher kitchen, Gerda's mother carefully, and so innocently, unpacked the food, placed it on plates, and offered it first, as a matter of respect, to her father-in-law. To Reb Weissmann.

Reb Weissmann who, throughout his entire life, had eaten only absolutely, strictly kosher food. Reb Weissmann, who endured near-starvation while imprisoned and while foraging bits of nourishment through his arduous journey home. And now, before him, a plate of chicken that certainly did not meet those exacting kosher standards.

As Gerda has written, "While the rest of the family looked on in speechless horror, Grandfather gazed at the daughter-in-law he had just met.

" 'That chicken looks very delicious, my dear daughter,' he intoned. With that, he went to wash his hands, recited a short blessing, and broke off a piece of the chicken."

And then he ate the chicken.

I've never heard a story quite like this one. I've read hundreds of accounts—I've witnessed many—where the opposite happens, reflecting the religious arrogance of the holier-than-thou.

Here, however, was a truly pious man who willingly risked his very life, throughout years of danger and depravation, rather than allow forbidden food to pass his lips.

Yet when an unanticipated choice suddenly confronted him, his response was immediate and clear. Nothing was more important to him than his new daughter-in-law's dignity. Nothing was more important to him than cementing the relationship between himself and this earnest and well-meaning young woman.

Gerda concludes, "With that story and a few others, my grandfather, whom I never met, became my lodestar in the bitterness, loneliness, and horror of the slave labor camps that I would endure as a young woman. If an old man could endure what he did, I reasoned, certainly I must, in his blessed memory, try to endure my own trials; and perhaps, like him, I, too, would be reunited with my family."

A magnificent story of piety and humanity, of a man who deeply believed that God makes stringent demands, demands that require sacrifice, hardship, dedication.

But more important than all of our religion's rules and regulations, more important than fulfilling the commandments to the letter, more important than all the piety, he believed in the duty—and the joy—of honoring and strengthening the family circle.

We don't label Jewish people "saints." But our past and present overflow with holy people, people whose lives and values and deeds inspire and amaze us.

Like an old man in a photograph from long ago, an old man with a long, untrimmed gray beard, a high *yarmulke*, clenched fists, a stern look across his face. And standing behind him, a daughter, her hand gently, affectionately resting on his shoulder.

Now we understand.

CHAPTER 25

Velvet Cushions

OWENSBORO, KENTUCKY. HOME of annual speedboat races, the world's largest sassafras tree, and the last public execution in America.

But those are not the reasons I chose Owensboro as my final student pulpit in 1971. My last year at rabbinical school, I had pretty much the pick of the litter as to which small congregation I would serve for the High Holidays and twice-monthly weekend visits. I selected Owensboro because it had a three-star motel. It was a fairly new, round, eight-story affair with a decent restaurant on the top boasting a splendid view of—well—Owensboro, Kentucky.

I'm not ashamed to admit it: creature comforts were important to me, especially since the previous year found me serving the small Jewish community of Williamson, West Virginia. Every other Friday I drove through places like Saltpeter and Crum, West Virginia, and into Williamson, "The Heart of the Billion Dollar Coal Fields."

Back then Williamson offered a choice of accommodations: the hotel on the main street where I once discovered a cockroach underneath my potato chips, and the motel outside town. I usually opted for the latter, which boasted color television. I could even occasionally hear the audio when the coal trains were not rumbling past the rear of the building. Most of my meals were eaten at an up-from-poverty restaurant that Ethel Kennedy had visited a few years earlier. Dining was enhanced by the playing of a tape of Richard and Karen Carpenter. Over and over and over again.

I was ready for a change.

So I became the chief rabbi of Owensboro, Kentucky, serving its small but dedicated congregation during my final year at the seminary.

As I recall, there were probably all of 20 Jewish families in the entire area. They maintained a beautiful century-old wooden synagogue in the heart of town, and my responsibilities included conducting Sabbath services, officiating at baby namings (there were none), bar and bat mitzvahs (there were none), funerals (there were none) and weddings (actually did have one).

In addition, I "directed" the religious school. Classes were small. We met around the little desk in Dougie's bedroom, and Dougie was the class. Occasionally we invited Dougie's five-year-old twin brothers in for an assembly.

Those were the days when my classmates and I were cutting our rabbinical teeth, engaging in what we used to call "hit-and-run Judaism" to the general delight and occasional consternation of small, remote Jewish communities we served.

When Hanukkah rolled around, I decided that although the entire Jewish child population of Owensboro consisted of Dougie, the twins, and three other pre-schoolers, they still deserved the best. So I purchased Cookie Monster and Oscar the Grouch hand puppets, and when we reached the time for the sermon during Friday night services, I crouched down behind the lectern and put on a mini-play starring the renamed "Hanukkah Candle Monster." It was a hit. Adorable.

That night was also the only time during my year in Owensboro when a visiting church group came unannounced.

I still recall the earnestness on the face of the teenage guest who approached me during the reception afterward. Tie askew, carrying a plate bearing a half-eaten jelly donut, he inquired, "So, rabbi. Do y'all worship the puppets every week?"

These little communities were the laboratories in which we learned to teach and preach and counsel. And if we were at all smart, we also learned to listen.

During those Saturday afternoons at his home, when his three energetic sons weren't monopolizing the conversation, Dougie's father and I developed a friendship that revolved around amiable banter but occasionally turned into earnest discussions of serious topics. One day Ed told me something rather personal. It was hardly a confession or a recounting of some horrible misdeed. But I could tell by the way he built up to the subject that he needed to discuss something important.

Ed told me that he simply didn't feel comfortable at our services at the synagogue. It just wasn't right for him. He wasn't getting what he really needed.

The type of worship wasn't the problem. Ed was raised in a big-city synagogue, reading from the same prayerbook, listening to the same melodies, following the same customs we used in Owensboro. He enjoyed the sermons I delivered, liked me and my predecessors, and felt as much a part of the Jewish community as any relative newcomer would.

No, it was something else. Something Ed was almost embarrassed about.

The seats.

Ed didn't like the seats. The charming old Owensboro synagogue accommodated worshippers in shiny white wooden pews. They seemed comfortable enough, and certainly fit in with the 19th century look of the sanctuary.

But to Ed, the wooden seats were just not right. Ed had a treasure of positive memories of growing up in his congregation in Syracuse. One of his fondest, and one of the most tactile as well, was sitting in the long services as a child and rubbing his hand back and forth, back and forth, across the velvet seat cushion next to him.

When he shared his secret, Ed almost winced. I think he expected me to scold him. Instead, I thanked him. His "confession" was a very vivid confirmation of the power of childhood memories. Rilke speaks of the same phenomenon in his *Letters to a Young Poet:* "And even if you were in some prison the walls of which let none of the sounds of the world come to your senses–would you not still then have your childhood, that precious, kingly possession, that treasure house of memories? Turn your attention thither. Try to raise the submerged sensations of that ample past."

For Ed, the comforting and precious sensation of those velvet seat cushions was exactly what Rilke described.

What is ironic is that some day, perhaps even now, as Dougie and his brothers are finding their way in the world, a velvet synagogue seat cushion may seem an aberration; only the cool, smooth feel of glossy varnished wood might truly bring back the sweet memories of growing up Jewish. Gliding a hand along a smooth surface may form a precious part of their "submerged sensations of that ample past."

The fact is, some of the most trivial elements of our past are personal echoes that ought not be ignored.

Velvet cushions do not form a religious identity. But wherever we can recollect sounds, and smells, and sights, and even textures of profound moments, we should embrace them. They may never be re-created, but their memory can often provide a salve for difficult times, or just a fleeting re-connection that, for a brief time, warms our spirit.

CHAPTER 26

Repairing the World

A BUS DRIVER with an infectious sense of humor just might change the course of human history. Here's how.

It was a dreary, bone-chilling, rainy morning outside O'Hare Airport. I joined a motley group of passengers eagerly scanning the circulating rental car buses, knowing that no matter which company I had chosen that day, two or three of the buses of the other agencies would make pick-ups before mine arrived.

As we waited and watched, a man, probably in his mid-forties, and in need of an ear, began to bend mine. He was in the midst of a frustrating trip that included a delayed flight, a missed connection, and a very important meeting that was, at that moment, being held without him. Not a happy camper. So he scowled. And griped. And let loose with one of those typical grumpy traveler's rants.

Our bus finally edged up to where we stood, the doors opened, we clambered aboard into soothing heat and bright lights. Once we pulled away from the curb, the driver, surprisingly, an older woman, looked back at us and called out, "Well, babies, welcome to my big yellow and black chariot. You just relax, take off your shoes if you want, put your feet up! For the next seven minutes, you are my honored guests."

Most of the passengers laughed, and even that angry, frustrated fellow had to smile. His tension seemed to evaporate.

A few minutes later, the bus pulled into the lot, and we scattered to locate our cars.

When I find myself part of a small event like this, I'm often aware that I'm witnessing, in action, a philosophy based on what one of my teachers called "the enduring possibility of being." We relate to God, Rabbi Reines suggested, in the way we affect the next second of the universe's existence.

For us human beings, our every word, our every action, for good or for evil, positive or negative, has a bearing on that ongoing act of the creation of the universe.

All of which brings us back to the rental car bus.

In my imagination, I envisioned that this amusing little incident—the driver's sweet, funny, graceful greeting—set off a series of reactions: That grouchy traveler was able to cope better with his frustrations. Later, when he called home, his own problems were not quite as overwhelming, and he felt relaxed enough to engage in some quality conversation with his eight-year-old daughter, further cementing their bond and adding to her sense of her own worth. And as a result of the support she received from her father, this child will now confidently realize her potential, becoming a career diplomat, and ultimately she'll resolve the crisis in the Middle East.

Far-fetched? Of course! Possible? Well, sure. And reason enough, in my view, to place ultimate importance on each and every one of our actions. When a stone is tossed into a pond, the ripples spread outward in all directions, eventually becoming invisible, but with movement and energy steadily stretching outward nevertheless. Our behavior, too, continually touches and influences the future, as we assume our roles in that ongoing act of creation.

The influence of our smallest act can be for evil or for good. It could initiate a series of consequences that will ultimately cause pain and suffering or, like the driver's amusing greeting, lend a calming perspective to an unpleasant time.

And when we do influence the future for the better, we become participants in what Judaism calls "*tikkun olam*," "repair of the world." *Tikkun olam* is not the exclusive domain of multi-millionaire benefactors or Nobel Prize winners, nor is it by any means exclusively Jewish. The process can be set in motion by each of us, in our unique, seemingly mundane ways.

Will a bus driver's unexpected interjection of caring and warmth and humor really bring peace to the Middle East?

Now, there's a stretch. Pie in the sky. How utterly far-fetched.

But you know, when you think about it, well ... It just might.

CHAPTER 27

How a Thick Wire and a Smart Lady Changed Our Lives

DRACULA WAS NOT amused.

Our very ordinary-looking but beloved brown tabby—his full moniker was "Cat Dracula," a name bestowed on him as a kitten by our then eight-year-old son—had ruled the family for twelve years, in three different homes, in two states.

He was a fine pussycat and even became a veteran traveler. Our "third child" regularly made the six-hour trip between Philadelphia and Vermont, usually curled in Sherri's lap, with one paw resting on my right forearm as I drove the car. We would place a small pan of kitty litter on the floor in the back seat. We soon discovered that for some reason the air in New Jersey always served, for Dracula, as a laxative.

The previous owner of our house in the Philadelphia suburbs had, at one time, rented the property to a couple equipped with the morality of fruit flies. When they moved out, they simply left their large orange cat, Caesar. Fortunately, one of the neighbors took pity on the abandoned cat and adopted him, but occasionally, after we arrived, Caesar became disoriented, tried to return to his now cat-friendly former home, and in so doing, encountered a definitely inhospitable Dracula. The orange fur on the lawn always served as a telltale sign.

Drack took no pleasure from invited animal visitors, either. After we made the permanent move to Vermont, Sherri's aunt and uncle arrived with their adorable little gray Schnauzer. Our cat instantly leapt onto the small dog's back, claws engaged. The poor, innocent pup had to be exiled to the car for the duration of the evening.

So there was a distinct absence of purrs and affectionate rubbing on the sunny January afternoon when Dracula first met his new housemate, his canine brother-to-be, our new dog, Giddy.

Giddy, or, more properly, Gideon (as if a dog knows his real name, or even cares), arrived with a convoluted, interesting background. We had been living in very rural Vermont for a couple of years and, even though Sherri's a native Vermonter, we felt like distinct outsiders. As we drove through town, we realized that ours was among the very few cars without a dog sitting in the front passenger seat, either leaning out the window on balmy days or rubbing a wet nose and drooling on the inside window during colder months. Oh, the shame.

Plus, since I travel fairly frequently, Sherri and I thought that a good-sized dog would provide both companionship and protection for Sherri and our daughter, then still in high school.

I guess people choose dogs similar to themselves, and since none of the Alpers consider themselves to bear fancy pedigrees (though we definitely are nice people), we decided that a mongrel, a young adult, one similar to Miracle, our son's fabulous shepherd-lab mix, would do just fine. We visited a few nearby kennels, and left word as to what we were seeking. Shouldn't be too hard a bill to fill.

Within a few weeks we received a call from the Bennington Kennel Club. They had precisely the dog we were looking for.

In fact, they had just received three dogs they were particularly eager to place. We headed south, leash in hand.

When we arrived, and before the dogs were brought out of the kennels for their "please take me home with you" parade, we learned that these three were victims of Hurricane Andrew, the storm that had devastated the area south of Miami five months earlier. Some pets were blown away as their homes were destroyed, while others had been surrendered by families forced to move temporarily into tents. Most had been living in crowded pounds for months, until volunteers organized "Andrew's Angels," flying dogs to kennels throughout the county, hoping for successful placements.

Thus briefed (and thoroughly softened up emotionally), we were ushered into a training room where the little procession commenced.

First out, a sort of dachshund mix, nervous, cute, wriggling against the arms of the shelter volunteer carrying her. Too small.

Next, a wiry gray terrier type was led out on a leash, looking frightened and fearful. No, we weren't interested. We'd wait to see contestant number three, the shepherd-lab mix that fit our requirements perfectly.

As soon as that final dog was led into the room, he took a quick look around, bolted to the side, and urinated on the wall. Some first impression. We stood by, confused, waiting for the shepherd-lab mix to emerge, wondering if there had been an error. This dog had neither shepherd nor lab in him; more of a combination of collie and golden retriever. He strutted about the place, sniffing everything, of course, happy to escape confinement, full of himself, a real take-charge guy. Cute. Very cute. About a year old, fifty-five pounds. With plenty of energy and self-confidence, he continually wore one of those open-mouth dog smiles, while wagging his tail with nearly lethal enthusiasm.

"Thanks, but we're not interested," I reported to the kennel director. "We have our hearts set on finding a dog just like our son's. We'll continue looking." This said as Sherri leaned down and began a one-way conversation with that third dog. Uh-oh.

Thirty minutes later, following the signing of papers outlining the care we promised to provide and our commitment to have our new pet neutered, the three of us headed north to our home. And to Dracula.

The introduction went something like this:

Giddy: "Hi. I'm the new pup in the family. Pleasure to meet you. How's about a sniff?"

Dracula: Hiss, hiss, spit, hiss, yowl, spit.

It never got better. Dracula, after all, was 12 years old and in no mood to change his settled ways. We sensed that from the moment the boys met, and it was confirmed a few days later when Giddy rounded a corner and surprised Dracula, lolling in the back yard. The cat bolted from his resting place, raced about 20 feet, and climbed the nearest tree. Which was me. In a split second he clawed his way up my body, ending up across my shoulders after putting a deep gouge in the highest branch, which throughout my life I have referred to as my nose.

Dracula spent many hours each day on the upper floors of our home, out of Giddy's way. Giddy, meanwhile, was acclimating himself to our home slowly. Very slowly.

Peeing on the wall of the kennel club should have been a tip-off that he wasn't fully housebroken. Giddy confirmed the suspicion immediately, and we went to work. Particularly helpful was a dog training video declaring that if a dog messes in the house, the best thing to do is to take a few sheets of newspaper, roll them up very tightly, and then smack *yourself* in the head. Because it's *your* fault! It went on to recommend proper timing for walks, and effective ways to reward good behavior. It worked for Giddy.

The primary problem we had with our new dog once again involved the cat. Cat poop, to be specific. It turns out, for dogs, cat excrement is a gourmet delicacy. We kept the kitty litter in the basement, which Giddy soon discovered, and in short order, his visits to what we eventually called "Giddy's buffet" became a regular part of his daily routine. We tried to intercept him, to yell "Bad dog!" whenever we could catch him in the act, but nothing seemed to work.

Dog breath is bad enough. Dog breath seasoned with cat poop? Beyond description. And a deal breaker.

Between his encounters with the cat, the slow progress in housebreaking, and then his raids on the litter box, Giddy had tipped the scales of my patience. I'm embarrassed to admit that I chose to throw in the towel. To bring him back to the kennel, surrender him and get an easier animal.

I called to report my decision and arrange a drop-off. Fortunately, the woman at the kennel club reacted not with anger or condemnation, but with patience. She asked about my reasoning, and I explained how the litter snacking was the last straw.

"I can't watch him all time," I moaned. "He's a smarty. Sneaks into the cellar when we're not looking and chows down."

The woman thought for a moment, then suggested, "Why not try this: Just latch the cellar door with a few inches of thick wire, so it's open wide enough for the cat, but not for the dog." Which we did.

Giddy turned out to be one of the world's premier dogs. A few years later, shortly after Dracula died, we brought Giddy to the animal shelter so he could pick out his own kitten. Giddy got along marvelously with Floyd and our later addition, Al (full name "Al Purr.") Dracula is buried in our garden, and, out of respect for their relationship, Giddy is buried up on the hillside. His small marble plaque reads:

Giddy
1992 – 2006
Golden tail held high, sniffing the wind.

We adore our splendid new dog, Barney, who gets along well with the cats. Occasionally he'll chase one under a table, but the moment he stops, the cat will emerge to give Barney a gentle nuzzle. We often think of Giddy, blessing his memory and feeling gratitude for all the happiness he gave us through the years.

And we remark to one another how amazing it is that years and years of such joy hinged on one tiny bit of wisdom, one somewhat obvious though overlooked solution, one very small act: a five-inch piece of wire that partially closed a cellar door.

Giddy and Bob
Photo by Hubert Schriebl

CHAPTER 28

Movie Tickets

I SHOULD BE used to it by now.

It seems that whenever I leave the frigid north to spend a day or two in Florida, it rains. That Monday in February was no different. And so I found myself waiting in line at a modern multiplex cinema in Fort Lauderdale, beneath my umbrella, about to buy a ticket to the matinee. Glad I packed all that sunscreen.

Ahead and behind me stood small groups of chattering people, men wearing plaid shorts and hearing aids, women, curiously, mostly Scandinavian. Either that, or someone was making a real killing in the area's gray-to-blonde hair coloring salon.

The line edged forward, slowly, until I finally reached the window. I announced my choice of movies and requested a single ticket. The young man looked at me and asked, "Senior?" It was then that I noticed on the price board behind the desk, "Adults: $8.50. Seniors, 60 and over, $6.50."

His question launched me into an unanticipated life cycle event. Three weeks earlier, I had crossed a critical threshold, not all pleased with the idea of starting my seventh decade. On the weekend of my birthday, Sherri had arranged a mystery trip in which we ended up walking into a beautiful condo at a ski resort where our daughter and son awaited. We spent a lovely few days doing activities that helped me avoid thinking about the reality of the existential transition I was undergoing.

But now: a movie theater. "Senior" ticket. It felt like a hammer to the head.

Quick answer required. The line behind me was long, the drizzle turning to rain, previews about to hit the screen. And I had a feeling that even a momentary hesitation on my part would draw constructive criticism from the impatient patrons at my back.

"Senior?"

I lied. It's as simple as that. I told an absolute fib. "No," I said, "not yet." I lied, paid $8.50, and walked into the theater as an under-60. I guess at that moment I was just not ready to own up to my age.

~

Not long after, a contrasting event took place in my hometown theater. "Village Picture Shows Cinema" is a perfect name for our ancient, two-screen movie house. It's been there forever, in various states of repair over the years, and the current owners try hard to present current hits mixed, occasionally, with eclectic small film festivals. Other than occasional nights during peak ski season, the place is never crowded, which is not always a blessing. Laughter is infectious, making it tough to watch comedies with only four others spread throughout the room.

Sherri and I went to see a film on a quiet Sunday evening. On one screen, a teenage vampire movie of some sort, and on the other, one of those films Sherri likes, featuring sad women weeping as they walk slowly through the moors. I bailed out after about half an hour of cinematic torture while Sherri and our friend Clare remained.

Before I left to kill time at the grocery store, I hung out for a while, talking with the manager and the guy who sold the addictive movie popcorn. All 25 patrons were nestled in their theaters, and the lobby was quiet. Until the door from the vampire movie opened, momentarily disgorging overwrought actors' screams. Just as quickly, when the door closed, the sounds once again became, thankfully, muffled.

A thin, young, rather frail looking girl walked hesitantly toward the three of us. She held some money in her hand. The popcorn seller began moving to his station, ready to wait on her so she could return quickly without missing part of what the producers no doubt, quite generously, called "the plot."

But the girl ignored the refreshments, and instead, approached the ticket counter where the manager and I were standing. Her pace was slow, her eyes downcast. When she reached us, she lifted her hand in which she gripped two folded dollar bills. Not quite crying, but visibly upset and nervous, she spoke in a soft voice. "I'm not eleven. I'm twelve. Here's the rest of the money I should have paid for my ticket."

Total silence for a few seconds. Then the manager and I both spoke, nearly at the same time, saying nearly the same thing. "You are a terrific kid. This was a hard thing to do. We wish more people were as honest as you." The manager good-naturedly argued with her, refusing to take her two dollars while she, visibly relieved and still shy, tried to insist. The manager won, and with a sweet, little smile, the girl returned to her friends in the seats and to the vampires on the screen.

It took a moment before the manager and the popcorn guy and I could resume our conversation, so taken were we by what we had just seen. It was restorative, reaffirming, and memorable. We witnessed a conflicted adolescent, ultimately doing the right thing, the moral thing. We also witnessed a child who was well on her way to becoming a woman of quality.

CHAPTER 29

The Wedding Photographer

WHEN A HISTORY of humankind is written, let's say, a hundred or two hundred years from now, wedding photograph albums will be a just a blip.

Think of it: for centuries, family lineages were maintained through carefully penned entries in heirloom Bibles, to be passed from generation to generation. With the advent of still photography, formal portraits of brides and grooms became the rage, followed, during the past few generations, by black and white snapshots, and then full color wedding albums.

Those big glossy pictures are still being produced, but along with them, and ultimately replacing them, are digital albums. No doubt within a short time there'll be something even more sophisticated, perhaps three-dimensional, virtual reality packages. Those wedding albums of still portraits will become a charming piece of history.

But wedding albums and the photographers who created them paralleled my sojourn here on earth, and they still have a central place in many lives. A friend of mine once shared with me snippets of the conversations that always seemed to go on in his house when the wedding photos were trotted out during family reunions.

"Oh my God. Look at Herbie with hair! Do you believe it? And those glasses on Aunt Selma! She never did have much of a fashion sense."

Or, as pages are flipped, and the group shots begin to appear, the clucking begins. "He's dead." "She's dead." "Look at how thin she was." And so on.

Photos help us remember. They're an important piece of every family's history.

I tried to keep that in mind when officiating at weddings. The photos are of great significance. The photographer has a job to do: sure, to earn a decent living, but also, in the larger scheme of things, to supply the bride and groom with a special treasure that they'll pass down through the generations.

Sometimes tension would arise between the photographer, who wanted to produce the best shots, and me, committed to creating for the couple a warm, memorable wedding. I considered those ceremonies to be sacred events, not press conferences. So I would carefully instruct the photographers: "While people are processing and recessing down and back up the aisle, you may do whatever you like, and when the couple reaches me, I'll pause so you can take a shot before we begin. But during the ceremony itself, no flash. No moving about the room. You're welcome to take available light shots, but only from the rear."

And frankly, the professionals understood. They'd cooperate. And the couple would end up with lovely photographs. Sometimes, we would even re-stage some poses under the wedding canopy immediately after the guests had left the room.

I've officiated at hundreds of weddings. Some, I remember very well. Many I've forgotten. Usually, of course, it's the bride and groom I recall. But there's one wedding that took place years ago—and not only can I not conjure up the faces or names of the couple, but, much as I try, I can't really seem to pinpoint if it took place during my days in Philadelphia, or, perhaps, while I served a congregation in Buffalo.

Yet, I remember the photographer, and what happened that night. I remember the photographer very well.

I don't think I ever knew his name. He was just one more guy with a camera and a bag of equipment appearing among the crowd of caterers and musicians and florists and others who operate on the periphery of a wedding.

I arrived, as always, thirty minutes prior to launch time. The picture taking was running late. Not unusual. I could work my way around it. I chatted with the groom's relatives while the couple and the bride's family were posing, then with the bride's relatives while the couple and the groom's family were similarly involved.

The guests all were seated and restive, and the string quartet was already playing some of their music a second time. We were now officially late. I tried to move things along. Signed the *ketubah* and civil license, watched everyone line up, and made sure there was wine in the *kiddush* cup.

I hadn't really noticed the photographer. He was a new guy, new to me, at least, and sort of prowled around these final preparations. I was about to weave my way through the tuxedos and gowns to tell him my policies when the harried wedding coordinator signaled the musicians and sternly directed me to walk to the *chuppah*. Which I did, without getting to the photographer.

No problem. This had happened many times before. I had a simple, effective way of handling such situations: a brief announcement was all that was necessary, something I'd often done when I hadn't had time to prepare the photographer or when I'd encounter a bevy of guests with cameras in their hands.

"Ladies and gentlemen," I said in a soft, composed voice, "in order to preserve the solemnity of these moments, I would ask that no flash pictures be taken until the conclusion of the ceremony." Everyone always complied.

And that's how I began this particular wedding, with the announcement for the benefit of the guests and especially for the benefit of the photographer who was at that moment standing in the rear of the aisle.

Only something went wrong that night. Just as I completed the opening Hebrew blessings, a flash went off. I looked up to see the photographer, in his tuxedo, camera chest high, tiptoeing down a side aisle and preparing to set up another shot. I was annoyed.

And so, in a firm, subdued, yet not particularly unpleasant tone, I interrupted with the reminder, "Please, no flash pictures until the end of the ceremony."

Just as I began my address to the couple, from the right side of the room came another flash. I looked up, and there stood the photographer, off to the side of the second row, looking down at his equipment, re-setting his camera for what I figured would be yet another intrusion. Now I was angry, and I could sense that the members of the wedding party, too, were annoyed.

One more chance. If he does it one more time, that's it. I'm not going to allow this obnoxious guy to ignore what I'm saying and get away with this. He figures he'll sell more pictures and the heck with me. One more time and he's out.

A minute later, another flash.

I clenched my teeth. Then I did something I'd never done before, and never did again. I turned to the men's side of the wedding party and asked, "Would one of the ushers please escort the photographer from the room?"

And that's precisely what happened. For just a second I could see the confused look on the photographer's face, but he went out obediently. Guests' heads nodded in support of my action, and I felt further vindicated by a grateful pat on the arm from the bride's father. We continued with the ceremony, uninterrupted.

And then it was over. The breaking of the glass, the kiss, the spirited applause, the wiping of tears and the recessional. I followed the grandparents down the aisle, and when I reached the foyer I encountered the usual scene: more hugging, more tears, veils and ties being straightened, and the wedding coordinator trying in vain at first, and finally, with success, to line up the wedding party to receive the congratulations of their guests.

I went through the line first. I had another commitment that evening, and needed to depart fairly quickly. It was a lovely ceremony, they told me. "Just wonderful. And rabbi, we're sorry about that photographer. Glad you took care of him. What an obnoxious jerk."

That was it. Finished. Time to leave.

I gathered my robe and book, and walked from the foyer into the entrance lobby. And there he was. The photographer. He was sitting on a bench against the wall, fishing in his equipment bag, preparing, I guess, to resume his picture taking. I hadn't counted on this. I was in a hurry, and besides, I hate confrontations. I really wanted to avoid him. But there was no way. He sat next to the only exit, and I had to pass right by him.

He fiddled with his camera as I drew closer to him. Maybe he won't see me, I hoped. Maybe he'll keep on doing what he's doing until I pass through the door. But when I was about twenty feet away, he looked up, looked right at me, for just a moment, and our eyes met. Then, just as quickly, he lowered his eyes. It was too brief to read his expression. Anger? Maybe. Embarrassment? I sort of hoped so. Perhaps he was even sorry for what he had done. I walked ahead, purposefully.

I drew closer. His expression was more like that of a wounded puppy dog. That's what I decided. That's pretty much what I was thinking as I watched him from the corner of my eye. He continued to adjust the camera. And as he did, his head turned slightly, just slightly, in the direction of the exit door toward which I was heading.

And then I saw it. I hadn't noticed it before. How could I? I had never been that close to him, and besides, so much else had been going on. I hadn't seen it.

He turned his head, and for the first time I realized: he was wearing a hearing aid.

I felt an internal jolt go through me as I continued to walk toward the door. I could tell he wanted to avoid me as best he could, and now I wanted to avoid him as well. But he was trapped by where he sat, and I was trapped by the direction in which I had to go. I strode forward, eyes glued to the entrance-way, while the photographer simply swiveled his head from one side to the other. He turned so he would not be looking in my direction as I passed to his left and through the front door.

And as he turned, I could see, in his other ear, a second hearing aid.

I left the building. I never saw the man again.

But I remember that incident. I remember that man. And the question is, the thing that bothers me, the thing that some-times keeps me awake at night, the thing that sometimes haunts me, is this: how can I possibly say I'm sorry?

It wasn't intentional. I wasn't being arrogant or purposely nasty. I was doing my job, trying to protect the bride and groom, trying to keep the wedding sacred and lovely. And I didn't know that the man was handicapped.

But still—But still—By my actions, I caused pain for another person. I felt terrible. What I saw in a sideward glance didn't register quickly enough for me to stop and speak with him. At that moment I was still fuming, and in a hurry, and I imagine neither he nor I were in any mood to chat.

Decades later, I remember. And I always will.

It's been many years, yet I can still see him in my mind, sit-ting there on the bench, rummaging through his equipment bag, his eyes downcast, a sad expression on his face. Defeated.

What I'd like to do, what I'd really like to do, is find him some day. Find him some day and look him straight in the eye, close up, close enough for him to hear me clearly, or easily read my lips.

And say to him just this:

"I'm sorry."

CHAPTER 30

The Dentist

FROM THE TIME my wife was in the second grade, her mother was chronically mentally ill.

At age 52, my mother-in-law entered a nursing home, and over the next twenty-five years, her diagnoses ranged from schizophrenia to cancer to severe depression. What we did know was that she had seizures, was extremely paranoid and often combative, and could not walk on her own. Sherri and I cared for her, placing her in a succession of nursing homes near us, in Buffalo, in Philadelphia, and finally, Vermont.

Dorothy wore dentures, and frequently she would break them, or lose them, or flush them away. It meant a trip to a dentist who would accept Medicaid, or to a clinic if we were particularly desperate.

On one such occasion, Sherri took her mother to the Temple University Dental Clinic, where they offered low-cost care as part of the training program for their students.

Sherri remembers a large room, 50 chairs, 50 dental students, 50 patients, and many instructors. At one point it suddenly occurred to Sherri: her mother was the only patient not handcuffed to a chair. She hoped her mother wouldn't notice.

A few days later, Dorothy needed an adjustment for her dentures, as often happened. This time I picked her up and took her to the clinic, and this time the room was empty. No other patients, no supervisors. Just the one student who had treated Dorothy before, a second career man in his mid-40s, now a few weeks away from graduation. He had been willing to meet us on a non-clinic day in order to relieve Dorothy's discomfort.

I don't really remember if, ultimately, he solved my mother-in-law's problem of the moment. I think he did. I think he successfully made the needed adjustment.

But this is what I do recall in every detail: after the procedure, when we lifted my mother-in-law to place her back in her wheelchair, we discovered that her diaper had leaked all over the dental chair.

The dental student, as if it were the most natural, totally routine, mundane task, dried the chair, washed it down with disinfectant, and cleaned the floor. He performed this rather disgusting chore, while, for the entire time, maintaining eye contact with his patient, asking her questions, making small talk.

This kindly man ministered to a chronically ill, indigent, incontinent, certifiably crazy old lady. And he treated her with dignity. There was holiness in that big empty room. There was holiness radiating from that man's tenderness.

During the course of her long and horrible odyssey, my mother-in-law was ill in one way or another for fifty years, and lived in institutions of one sort or another for the last twenty-five. My wife and I encountered literally hundreds of caregivers. Most of the names and faces have long since faded from my memory, perhaps part of the way the mind adapts to pain and interminable sadness.

But I remember with admiration and gratitude that dental student at the Temple University Clinic. Not because of his scientific skill, not because of his artistry or his intellect.

But because of his remarkable decency.

CHAPTER 31

Becoming a Man

I BLAME IT on Stanley. If it weren't for him, none of this would have happened.

I was a few months shy of twelve when the planning for my bar mitzvah began in earnest. Since my birthday falls on January 29th, back in 1958, when I'd turn 13, the logical day for my big event was the following Sabbath, February 1st. The date was confirmed with the synagogue.

And then we learned about Stanley. Stanley, one of the richest boys in Providence and a member of another congregation, had scheduled his bar mitzvah for February 1st, too. We would compete for the same kid guests. Stanley's family planned a black tie (even for the children) gala celebration at a swank downtown hotel, while the Alpers were set to host a synagogue luncheon reception with fancy sandwiches (no crusts) and hundreds of pastries my grandmother and mother baked at our home.

We caved in. My bar mitzvah took place on January 18th.

The bar mitzvah, and its female equivalent, the bat mitzvah, stand as one of Judaism's most ingenious contributions to child rearing. A pubescent girl or boy, on the threshold of life's most awkward developmental stage, studies for a time, learns to read Hebrew from the Torah, which he or she then does before a congregation of family and friends, few of whom have mastered the esoteric body of knowledge themselves. Afterward, congratulations and celebrations, which, if done well, imbue the child with a sense of accomplishment as well as the community's approval and support. Not a bad way to begin the very complex teenage years.

In my synagogue, the second and third rows would be filled with recent and upcoming bar and bat mitzvah kids, many of whom had a vested interest in making subtle facial expressions that would throw off the day's star. Especially during the reading of the Ten Commandments. The weekly repetition of the word "adultery" did not seem to be a problem, since, in this age group, its definition was mostly unknown. But in the very last commandment, as if a direct verbal gift from the comedy gods, comes the clear, microphone-enhanced recitation that one is forbidden to "covet thy neighbor's ass." It almost inevitably drew giggles.

I figured I could handle that element just as well as my friends who'd gone before me. Simply look over the hecklers' heads, mumble the word, and move on quickly to the next prayers.

For me, the real test came when reading from the prophets.

About a year before the big event, I met with Selig Salkowitz, our warm and affable rabbi.

Opening a book listing the weekly readings, he selected for me verses from Exodus and a corresponding section from one of the prophets. Then he handed me a thin brown volume of Hebrew and dictated my assignment, which I dutifully wrote on the inside cover.

I've sometimes wondered if, growing up in Rhode Island, I ever had a New England accent. The brown book provides the answer. I had written "Exodus 7:14-29" and "Jeremier 31:1-17." Apparently, I did.

When I got home I immediately read the English translations. No problem with the words from Exodus, but when I read what was in "Jeremier," I panicked. There, right there in Chapter 31, verse 4, the word "virgin!" I was supposed to read the word "virgin" out loud, directly in front of Robin and Joey and Sammy and the two Rickeys and Cori and Larry.

It got worse. "Virgin" was repeated in verse 13.

And to think: Stanley, whose bar mitzvah took place on what should have been my date, didn't have any of these problems.

As it happened, my anxiety about the requirement to read "ass," "virgin" and "virgin" in front of my friends and hundreds of adults turned out to be the lesser of my concerns during that run-up to my big day. Another issue loomed larger. I needed to make a major decision.

The way it worked in those old, pre-liberation days, my mother and grandmothers sat proudly in the front row, while the chubby little focus of the morning graced the pulpit, my father on one side and my grandfather on the other.

Here was the dilemma: ours was a family of men who kissed. Each other. No problem there. Who's watching the entranceway to a house, or inside a car, or a dining room right after the Sabbath blessings have been recited?

But the bar mitzvah was different. A whole congregation of people, including my not-uncritical pubescent friends. For months I debated: Should I kiss my father and my grandfather, right up there on the pulpit, right in front of everybody? Or was it time now to revert to a manly, clenched-jawed handshake? (This was in 1958, by the way, before masculine hugs had been invented.)

Despite seriously considering racing out the back exit mid-ceremony, I made it through the entire service. Read my Hebrew portions with a few errors, got through the English translations with their embarrassing mentions of "ass" and "virgin," and stood face to face with Rabbi Salkowitz at the front of the pulpit as he delivered his blessing to me. I recall both his very meaningful words and the little droplets of saliva he projected onto my glistening, pre-acne forehead.

He finished, then shook my hand.

As we had rehearsed, I returned to my seat and sat down. Big grin. It was over. A success.

And then I did what I guess I had known I would do all along. I kissed my grandfather. Then I kissed my father. Somehow, I can't help feeling that more than any other elements of that day, my real ascent to manhood, or to the kind of man I hope I've become, began the moment I kissed my grandfather and my father.

Twenty-seven years later. My own son's bar mitzvah. Both his mother and I sat with him on the pulpit, and a colleague conducted the service. That day my more important role was as a father, not rabbi. But toward the end of the service I did opt to bless Zack, quietly, privately, before the open ark. And after I whispered "Amen," without hesitation, with no second thoughts, he reached up to me, for a big hug and kiss, right there in front of 400 people.

Life had come full circle.

CHAPTER 32

Laugh in Peace

THE FACT THAT 2,000 Muslims were laughing at me, a rabbi, might have been cause for concern. Except that I'm also a full-time stand-up comic. And I was appearing at Muslim-fest, in Toronto, on a summer night a few years ago.

It's been a pretty fascinating journey, this transition from serving as a full-time rabbi, a natural and very rewarding career choice, to performing as a full-time stand-up comic, a vocation that never entered my wildest dreams. And yet, these two seemingly opposite careers are totally compatible if, as I certainly do, one appreciates the spiritual nature of laughter.

In many respects it's been a roller coaster ride, with some achingly memorable lows and totally unanticipated, exhilarating highs along the way.

I can still feel the churning in my stomach as I stood in a lobby, peering out the entrance window of a dank Reading, Pennsylvania, restaurant. Inside the dining room, temporarily converted to a comedy club, the opening act was struggling to keep the attention of the late night, heavily drinking crowd. I was up next.

Watching the torrents of rain wash over the parking lot, I mentally rehearsed my few good jokes over and over. I figured that the vehicles parked against the building might give me a sense of the kind of audience awaiting this earnest rookie comic with five months experience. A hint came when I spotted a colorful sticker affixed to the rear window, beneath a gun rack, on a muddy pick-up truck: "If you drive too close, I'll flick a booger on your windshield." Uh oh. Will it be possible, I wondered, that these folks might somehow appreciate the cerebral, clean, sophisticated humor of a rabbi/comedian? They did not.

Eliciting smiles and laughter can be a complex phenomenon. A well-known author once told me it was only when he sat in the back of a movie theater, watching, for the first time, as one of his stories came to life on the screen, that he could finally gauge the effectiveness of his humor through the audience's laughter. Live stand-up is the polar opposite, providing instant feedback to the performer. When a joke fails, we call it dying. But when a joke works, when in response to our words people immediately smile and laugh and wipe away tears, that's nothing short of divine.

I've been blessed with many of those moments, but one event in particular stands out, not only because of the pure thrill of making people laugh but, in this case, for what it says about the way shared joy affects humanity, and community, and possibility: Toronto's Muslimfest.

What was a rabbi doing there? It was a natural outgrowth of performing over 250 shows with Muslim comedy partners, something that began at a Philadelphia synagogue in April, 2002, and has since spread to dozens of other synagogues, churches, mosques, theaters, and, most importantly, to college campuses from Oregon to Boston.

The Muslimfest show was unique—and just a bit daunting. I took the stage, surveyed the audience, and confessed, "I feel really strange here. So alone. Such an outsider. Think of it: all of you... all of you are... uh...Canadians! And I'm American." The theater rocked with laughter and applause, and my set was launched.

Bob and Ahmed

My Muslim colleagues include Ahmed Ahmed, of Egyptian background; Azhar Usman, of Indian background, and Mo Amer, a Palestinian born in Kuwait. We do Muslim-Jewish shows, frequently enhanced by the addition of a Baptist minister, Rev. Susan Sparks. And we have so much fun at each performance, it's almost criminal.

We call our shows "Laugh in Peace."

Back in late 2001, Ahmed and I were brought together as a gimmick by a savvy publicist. Our relationship quickly developed into a friendship based on the camaraderie of fellow artists and the breezy banter of guys who really enjoy one another's company. We laugh together a lot. Like the night following a show at a suburban Chicago synagogue, when we drove downtown to a blues bar. Ahmed was on his cell phone, so I entered and told the cashier I'd pay the cover fee for myself and my friend, who would arrive shortly.

"Fine," he said. "What's his name?"

"Ahmed," I replied.

"What's his name?"

"Ahmed," I repeated.

Which received the somewhat condescending response, "I know you're Ed. What's *his* name?"

Later, when Ahmed began to focus more on acting and international comedy venues, I started to work with Azhar. Raised in the very Jewish Chicago suburb of Skokie, Azhar tells synagogue audiences, "I'm more Jewish than you are. I've got the beard going. I keep strictly kosher. And, I went to law school."

Mo and I work together often, including a show at Congregation Kol Ami, in White Plains, N.Y. On the way back to the hotel, Mo inquired, "By the way, Bob. What does 'Kol Ami' mean?"

"It's Hebrew for 'Voice of my people,'" I replied.

"Oh," he said. "Because in Arabic, it means 'eat my uncle.'"

When Susan performs with us, she proudly compares for the audience her inclusive, liberal American Baptists with the more fundamentalist Southern Baptist denomination, noting that in her group, women are allowed to dance and to preach, though usually not at the same time. Her email signature proclaims "Baptist—Just Not Like You Expect."

Our shows are absolutely non-political. In every performance, each of us does a solo set, and then we sit together onstage, telling road stories from our travels across North America and England. For example, our discovery about how similar churches, synagogues, and mosques can be: in most of those places, the earnest lay leaders don't have a clue where the light switches are or how to operate the sound systems. We describe visits to each other's homes: the women in my small Vermont town fell in love with Ahmed and continually pester me for updates on his life. While eating dinner at Ahmed's parents' home in California, Ahmed's dad asked about my family. When I told him my wife would be having shoulder surgery the following month, he looked gravely at me and ordered, "You must stop twisting her arm!"

Of all we do, it's the college shows that never cease to amaze us. Like the evening at the University of Pennsylvania, where Ahmed and I were introduced to the audience by three students, presidents of the co-sponsoring organizations of Jews, Muslims, and Arabs. From the stage we looked out on a standing room only crowd of smiling, laughing faces, many of the males wearing yarmulkes, many of the females wearing hijabs. At the University of Arkansas it occurred to us that we were guests of "the razorbacks." Thus, a Muslim and a Jew, performing at a school whose mascot is a pig. Go figure.

And finally, the night when Azhar and I did a show at Georgia Tech. We were hosted by the presidents of the Jewish Student Union and the Muslim Students Association. Azhar and I could easily infer that these two leaders were close friends. And so we were deeply moved when they told us how, though their offices were next door to one another in the Student Union, until they began working on "Laugh in Peace," they'd never, ever spoken to one another.

No question, "Laugh in Peace" was conceived initially as a way to further our comedy careers, to book more gigs, to raise our visibility. It would be disingenuous to suggest anything else. But as the act and our personal relationships evolved, we quickly understood how "Laugh in Peace" brought a sense of hope and relief and healing that shared laughter—especially shared laughter between communities in frequent tension— can provide.

Not everybody loves us, alas. Occasional self-righteous practitioners of each faith are not amused, attacking us as heretical. Frankly, when we think of them, a term coined by the social organizer Saul Alinsky comes to mind: "Intellectually constipated." We can't please everyone.

But for most, a Muslim, a Christian, and a Jew doing comedy together and demonstrating their friendship clearly represents the kind of unity in diversity that is part and parcel of America's blessed uniqueness. And this we know for certain: when people laugh together, it's very difficult to hate one another.

It all comes down to this: University of California, Riverside campus. Tensions had risen on campus after a few hate-filled slogans were written across some signs affixed to bulletin boards. And then Ahmed, Susan, and I appeared for our show. Full house. The co-sponsoring Muslim kids, Jewish kids, and Christian kids set up extra seats, collected tickets, ushered, introduced us from the stage, laughed, applauded, and chowed down at the reception. Together. Bonding through shared laughter.

And more than once that night, Susan, Ahmed and I heard these delicious words: "Thanks. We Needed That."

Also by
Rabbi Bob Alper

Books

A Rabbi Confesses (color cartoon book)
Life Doesn't Get Any Better Than This

CDs

Bob Alper: Rabbi/Stand-Up Comic (Really)
Guaranteed Funny: 101 Totally Clean Jokes

DVD

What Are You, A Comedian?

All items available through www.BobAlper.com

About Rabbi Bob Alper

"SURE. BUT THIS might take a while," is how Bob Alper responds when the passenger flying next to him asks what he does. He's a rabbi who earned a doctorate at Princeton Theological Seminary, has performed stand-up comedy hundreds of times with Arab and Muslim comedians, and is heard daily on the Sirius/XM clean comedy channel. Bob is also an author who adores living in rural Vermont with his wife Sherri, a psychotherapist, a pair of affectionate but annoying geriatric cats, and Barney, a loveable rescue dog from Puerto Rico who ignores commands in both English and Spanish. Bob's unique experiences, from leading large congregations to performing stand-up at Toronto's "Muslimfest," make for a wealth of gentle stories that touch people of all backgrounds with warmth, humor, and wisdom. His earlier collection, *Life Doesn't Get Any Better Than This: The Holiness of Little Daily Dramas* was described by a Detroit Free Press reviewer as "a volume of spiritual gems." Bob continues telling stories in his signature style in this new book, *Thanks. I Needed That.*

Colophon

READ THE SPIRIT Books produces its titles using innovative digital systems that serve the emerging wave of readers who want their books delivered in a wide range of formats—from traditional print to digital readers in many shapes and sizes. This book was produced using this entirely digital process that separates the core content of the book from details of final presentation, a process that increases the flexibility and accessibility of the book's text and images. At the same time, our system ensures a well-designed, easy-to-read experience on all reading platforms, built into the digital data file itself.

David Crumm Media has built a unique production workflow employing a number of XML (Extensible Markup Language) technologies. This workflow allows us to create a single digital "book" data file that can be delivered quickly in all formats from traditionally bound print-on-paper to nearly any digital reader you care to choose, including Amazon Kindle®, Apple iBook®, Barnes and Noble Nook® and other devices that support the ePub and PDF digital book formats.

And due to the efficient "print-on-demand" process we use for printed books, we invite you to visit us online to learn more about opportunities to order quantities of this book with the possibility of personalizing a "group read" for your organization or congregation by putting your organization's logo and name on the cover of the copies you order. You can even add your own introductory pages to this book for your church or organization.

During production, we use Adobe InDesign®, <Oxygen/>® XML Editor and Microsoft Word® along with custom tools built in-house.

The print edition is set in Minion Pro and Avenir Next fonts..

Cover art and Design by Rick Nease: www.RickNeaseArt.com.

Editing by David Crumm.

Copy editing and XML styling by Henry Passenger and Dmitri Barvinok.

Digital encoding and print layout by John Hile.

If you enjoyed this book, you may also enjoy

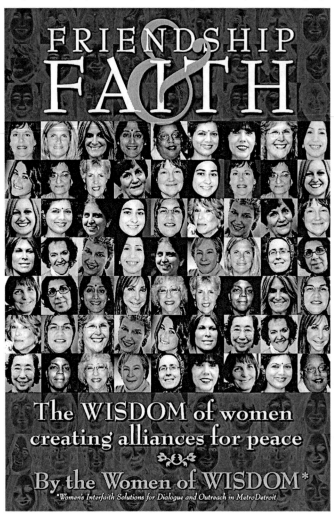

Finding a good friend is hard. Preserving a friendship
across religious and cultural boundaries—a challenge
we all face in our rapidly changing world—is even
harder.

http://www.FriendshipAndFaith.com

ISBN: 978-1-934879-19-1

If you enjoyed this book, you may also enjoy

"He's a little bit of Dave Barry, David Sedaris and that fun quirky guy you met on an airplane once all rolled into one." —*from a review on Amazon.com*

http://www.SpiritualWanderer.com

ISBN: 978-1-934879-07-8

If you enjoyed this book, you may also enjoy

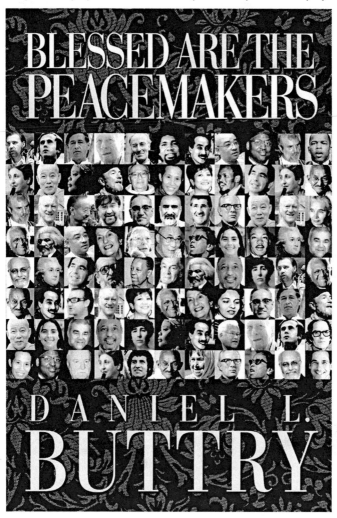

In the pages of this book you will meet more than 100 heroes. Watch out! Reading about their lives may inspire you to step up into their courageous circle.

http://www.BlessedAreThePeacemakers.info

ISBN: 978-1-934879-76-4

If you enjoyed this book, you may also enjoy

In *This Jewish Life: Stories of Discovery, Connection and Joy*, 55 voices enable readers to experience a calendar's worth of Judaism's strengths—community, healing, transformation of the human spirit and the influence of the Divine.

http://www.ThisJewishLife.com

ISBN: 978-1-934879-36-8

CPSIA information can be obtained
at www.ICGtesting.com
Printed in the USA
FSOW02n0311010417
32416FS

9 781934 879863